797,885 Books
are available to read at

Forgotten Books

www.ForgottenBooks.com

Forgotten Books' App
Available for mobile, tablet & eReader

ISBN 978-1-330-46304-8
PIBN 10030703

This book is a reproduction of an important historical work. Forgotten Books uses state-of-the-art technology to digitally reconstruct the work, preserving the original format whilst repairing imperfections present in the aged copy. In rare cases, an imperfection in the original, such as a blemish or missing page, may be replicated in our edition. We do, however, repair the vast majority of imperfections successfully; any imperfections that remain are intentionally left to preserve the state of such historical works.

Forgotten Books is a registered trademark of FB &c Ltd.
Copyright © 2015 FB &c Ltd.
FB &c Ltd, Dalton House, 60 Windsor Avenue, London, SW19 2RR.
Company number 08720141. Registered in England and Wales.

For support please visit www.forgottenbooks.com

1 MONTH OF FREE READING

at

www.ForgottenBooks.com

By purchasing this book you are eligible for one month membership to ForgottenBooks.com, giving you unlimited access to our entire collection of over 700,000 titles via our web site and mobile apps.

To claim your free month visit: www.forgottenbooks.com/free30703

* Offer is valid for 45 days from date of purchase. Terms and conditions apply.

Similar Books Are Available from
www.forgottenbooks.com

The Human Mind, Vol. 1 of 2
A Text-Book of Psychology, by James Sully

Dream Psychology
Psychoanalysis for Beginners, by Sigmund Freud

The Psychology of the Emotions
by Th. Ribot

An Introduction to Psychology
by James Rowland Angell

The Psychology of Beauty
by Ethel D. Puffer

The Psychology of Time, Historically and Philosophically Considered
With Extended Experiments, by Herbert Nichols

Psychology of the Nations
by A. Kip

Psychology of the Unconscious
by C. G. Jung

Graphology and the Psychology of Handwriting
by June Etta Downey

Psychopathology
by Edward J. Kempf

Educational Psychology
A Treatise for Parents and Educators, by Louisa Parsons Hopkins

Your Inner Self
by Louis Edward Bisch

The Psychology and Pedagogy of Anger
by Roy Franklin Richardson

Outwitting Our Nerves
A Primer of Psychotherapy, by Josephine Agnes Jackson

The Theory of Psychoanalysis
by C. G. Jung

Psychology from the Standpoint of a Behaviorist
by John B. Watson

The Unconscious the Fundamentals of Human Personality, Normal and Abnormal
by Morton Prince

Repressed Emotions
by Isador H. Coriat

The Blot Upon the Brain
Studies in History and Psychology, by William W. Ireland

The Psychology of Persuasion
by William Macpherson

PSYCHOLOGY
—OF—
SALESMANSHIP

BY

GEO. R. EASTMAN, A. B., A. M.

TEACHER IN STEELE HIGH SCHOOL
SECRETARY OF THE REX FILM RENOVATOR MFG. CO.

AUTHOR OF

PSYCHOLOGY OF BUSINESS EFFICIENCY
PSYCHOLOGY OF ADVERTISING
(IN PREPARATION)

"The master of the art of selling is the master of men"
—Psychology of Salesmanship

THE SERVICE PUBLISHING COMPANY
DAYTON, OHIO

COPYRIGHT, 1916
—BY—
GEO. R. EASTMAN

CONTENTS

FOREWORD

	Page
SELLING THE CONTENTS TO THE READER	7

INTRODUCTION

SALESMAN PERFORMS AN ECONOMIC FUNCTION	10
PRACTICAL KNOWLEDGE AND SKILL	11
SALESMANSHIP IS APPLIED PSYCHOLOGY	15

PART I

MAKING THE SALE

PREPARATION OF SALESMAN AND OF SELLING PLAN	16
PARTS OF THE SELLING PROCESS	16
PRE-APPROACH (Investigation and Preparation)	19
APPROACH AND SECURING ATTENTION	25
SOLICITATION	31
Aim of the Solicitation	31
Stating the Aim in Taking Up a New Point	36
Putting the Main Points in Writing	37
Adapting Solicitation to Customer's Mind	39
Effectiveness Cumulative	41
Brief Solicitation First	42
Renewal of the Solicitation	43
Truth	45
Demonstration	47
Arousing Irrelevant Impulses	50
Illegitimate Means	51
MAKING SOLICITATION EFFECTIVE	52
DIAGNOSIS	58

CONTENTS

DEALING WITH OBJECTIONS	67
MAKING KNOWN THE PRICE	74
FEELING OUT AND CLOSING	75
AFTER CLOSING	86
GENERAL CONSIDERATIONS	89
SALESMANSHIP AS A PROFESSION	92
PROBLEMS OF MARKETING COMMODITIES	94

PART II

PROCESS OF THINKING, FEELING AND ACTING	102
Behavior	102
Distinction between Mental and Physical Processes	102
Subjective and Objective Realms	103
METHOD OF GAINING PSYCHOLOGICAL KNOWLEDGE	105
EXPERIMENTAL PSYCHOLOGY	106
KNOWLEDGE OF THE MINDS OF OTHERS	107
CLASSIFICATION OF CONSCIOUS PROCESSES	108
MIND AND BRAIN	111
HABIT	111
ACQUIRING PROFICIENCY IN A NEW LINE	114
ASSOCIATION OF PROCESSES OF THINKING, FEELING, AND ACTING	117
Association by Contiguity	117
Association by Similarity	119
MEMORY AND THE ART OF RECOLLECTING	123
Association Processes in Education	128
PROCESS OF LEARNING	129
Learning Aims to Grasp the Significance of Things	132
Most Efficient Method of Learning	134
INTEREST AND ATTENTION	139
Voluntary and Spontaneous Attention	141
FOCUS AND MARGIN OF ATTENTION	145
Expectant Attention	146
Attention Determines Thinking, Feeling and Acting	148
ACTS OF WILL, OR IDEO-MOTOR ACTIVITY	150
Acts of Will Involving Deliberation	151

CONTENTS

THINKING 153
    Test of Truth 162
JUDGMENT AND REASONING 164
    Belief and Action 167

PART III

FACTORS WHICH DETERMINE THINKING, FEELING AND ACTING 169
INSTINCTS OR PREDISPOSITIONS 169
    Enumeration of Instincts 173
    Instincts Require Educational Development 177
    Modification of Instincts 180
WILL TO LIVE 182
    Instinct of Self-Realization 182
    Moral Interest 185
    Two Meanings of Interest 189
CLASSIFICATION OF INTERESTS 191
    Morality—the Major Interest 191
    Philanthropy Interest 194
    Politico-Legal Interest 195
    Family and Home Interest 195
    Sociability Interest 196
    Health Interest 197
    Education Interest 197
    Aesthetic Interest 197
    Wealth Interest 198
    Vocation Interest 199
    Work and the Need for Recreation 202
    Recreation Interest 204
CORRELATION AND CO-ORDINATION OF INTERESTS 208
INTEREST, DESIRE, VALUE AND PRICE 212
TRUTH, THE IDEAL OF SELLING 216
AWAKENING LATENT NEEDS 219
AROUSING DESIRE 220
SUGGESTION AND IMITATION 223
    Factors of Suggestibility 225

CONTENTS

Subconscious Imitation 231
Conscious or Intentional Imitation............................ 234
FULLY REASONED CHOICE AND DEMONSTRATED TRUTH........ 239
RATIONAL SUGGESTION AND RATIONAL IMITATION............... 241
Rational Suggestion 242
INCREASING THE EFFICIENCY OF THE SELLING FORCE......... 250
Convention of Salesmen.. 251
Sales Contest 252
Awakening Interest Increases Energy..................... 253
DEVELOPING CHARACTER AND PERSONALITY........................ 256
Success Depends upon Character............................. 256
Self Confidence 259
Personal Magnetism 261

FOREWORD

SELLING THE CONTENTS OF THIS BOOK TO THE SALESMAN WHO IS CONSIDERING WHETHER HE WILL BE REPAID FOR THE EFFORT REQUIRED TO MASTER IT.

This book is intended for the person who is convinced that salesmanship is an honorable profession, rendering an important and difficult service. It is for those who have awakened to the fact that the salesman is not born ready made, with his powers fully developed.

The salesman must be made, in large part at least, by serious study. The efficient salesman must know the workings of, and have skill in influencing complicated and intangible mental processes, which determine the behaviour of men. It takes persistent hard work to gain an understanding of the factors and processes which determine the actions of men. The salesman's efficiency will vary directly with this understanding.

The scientific farmer, the teacher, the accountant, the lawyer, the engineer, the architect, the physician, the minister, and many others, have found it well worth their while to make a serious and careful preparation for the practice of their profession. The salesman will at last come to realize that intelligent preparation for his work is quite as important, and will bring equally great reward.

The salesman can determine whether he is fully prepared for the practice of his profession by asking himself a few questions, and grading himself on his ability to answer them.

What is salesmanship? What does the approach aim to accomplish? What are the laws which govern the direction of attention to a thing, when it has once been secured? How is attention related to interest? What interests does the normal man have? Do you know to what interests your selling appeal should be directed? What is the relation between interest and desire? How would you undertake to arouse desire? When you have aroused desire, do you know how to carry it over into action? How can you tell when you have reached the "psychological moment" for attempting to close? How can a man think ahead and plan what he will say next, while his attention is adequately given to what he is saying? What are the best methods of learning, remembering, and thinking?

This book aims to give the salesman scientific knowledge which will enable him to answer satisfactorily the foregoing, and many other similar questions. Scientific knowledge is thorough and consistent. Methods guided by such knowledge are efficient in accomplishing the desired result. A scientific knowledge of mental processes enables the salesman to work intelligently and directly toward the end he wishes to achieve, instead of resorting to the aimless and wasteful try, try again of the man whose knowledge is not equal to the demands of the situation.

The salesman ought not to be discouraged, or condemn this book, if he does not at once grasp the full significance or practical helpfulness of all it contains. Two or more thoughtful readings may be required to enable one to get the psychological point of view and master the method of the science. One has not mastered this discussion in a way that will make it of the greatest practical helpfulness until he understands clearly all the parts, and perceives their relations to each other and to the whole. He must learn to reassemble and to put to working harmoniously together the various processes that are here knocked down and taken apart for purposes of study.

The writer has tried long and earnestly to make this book elementary and practical. He is convinced that he could make it simpler only at the expense of making it more superficial. This would defeat the end aimed at in preparing it. The difficulty encountered in understanding and applying what is written here results mainly from the intangible nature of the subject matter and the lack of skill in exploring one's own mental processes. As one becomes skilled in the exploration of his own mind, the practical usefulness of the principles discussed here will become apparent.

INTRODUCTION

SALESMAN PERFORMS AN ECONOMIC FUNCTION

AS A FACTOR in the world of business the salesman is concerned with effecting a mutually advantageous exchange, in which money, or some other means of securing satisfaction, or some form of satisfaction, is received in return for the service, or serviceable thing sold. As the salesman performs an important business function, he should have some knowledge of business affairs.

The salesman must be master of his merchandise. He should have adequate knowledge of the materials, and mechanical and industrial processes employed in making the articles he sells. He must clearly perceive what the process of manufacture confers on the article, in giving to it qualities which make it have a commercial value superior to other things with which it may come into competition. It is generally recognized that it is important for the salesman to have knowledge of these things which may be called the material factors in salesmanship.

A man may be well informed in regard to the things previously mentioned and still be very poorly equipped in salesmanship. Additional factors which make for success, are knowledge of what to do in attempting to sell, and why it is done; also skill in doing it. Skill may be developed best by practice in which one's efforts are guided by knowledge of the "what" and the "why." It is the purpose of this book to help to give a knowledge of the what to do, and why to do it.

PRACTICAL KNOWLEDGE AND SKILL

The art of selling may be acquired by blind imitation of other's methods of selling and by more or less haphazard methods of trial and error. The methods that fail are rejected and the methods that succeed are adopted, without knowing why they fail or succeed.

By this process one may gain considerable knowledge of what to do and may become skillful in doing it. But he will be able to apply this knowledge and skill only under the conditions in which he learned to apply them. They are not readily transferable and adaptable to a different situation.

Knowledge and skill acquired by the method of blind trial and error afford satisfactory guidance only in cases easily recognized as similar to those in which success has been achieved previously. One who has learned by this method will not be able to perceive the circumstances which alter cases. Even if he perceived them, he could adapt his knowledge and skill to the requirements of the altered circumstances, only by continuing the process of selecting the lucky hits from the misses.

Such a process of acquiring knowledge and skill

lacks the guiding light of intelligence. Even when one has gained practical success by this method he does not know why one attempt succeeded and the other failed.

One who has previously acquired the knowledge which enables him to understand the whys and wherefores of success will be able to go intelligently about the task of finding the right course of procedure under novel circumstances. If one has this kind of knowledge, when it occurs to him to try various lines of effort, he will be able to forecast more or less accurately the consequences of each line of action. He will thus be able to avoid much wasteful bungling.

The Theory of Salesmanship endeavors to bring into clear consciousness a knowledge of the *whats* and the *hows*, the *whys* and the *wherefores* of the art of selling. It aims to formulate general principles and to organize them into a system so that they will have the greatest practical usefulness in selling. It aims, not at a theory divorced from practice, but at a system of general principles which will furnish helpful guidance to the various practical activities of the salesman.

In this book the process of selling is carefully analyzed. A theory of salesmanship is developed so that the salesman can see the general principles which are to be applied in efficient selling. The salesman will master his art more quickly and will become more expert in it by learning and applying these general principles.

The knowledge and skill which enable one to do a thing have a certain value. But unless one knows why he does the thing that way, he can not adapt his knowledge and skill to altered conditions which make it necessary to change the way of doing the thing. He can not adapt his knowledge and skill to doing other things.

One who knows why he does a thing in the way he does, and sees that the doing is a particular application of general principles, can do many other things which come under the same general principles. A knowledge of the general principles of selling makes one resourceful and adaptable.

The salesman who understands the general principles of salesmanship can instruct and direct others in selling. He has the sort of knowledge which helps the salesman to develop into a salesmanager.

SALESMANSHIP IS APPLIED PSYCHOLOGY

Why is it profitable for the salesman to study psychology? Salesmanship is an art. Though the salesman performs an economic function, the principles of his art are psychological. In the act of selling, the salesman deals directly with mental processes. Salesmanship is, essentially, applied general, individual, and social psychology.

Salesmanship is the ability to influence the mental processes of a person so that he will desire the service, or the serviceable thing, offered to him and will perform the acts necessary to secure it. The art of selling involves applying to a special line of activity, under the conditions which govern there, the general principles which must be applied in any case in which one person seeks to influence the behaviour of another.

The art of salesmanship involves understanding of, and skill in influencing the mental processes which are the factors that determine the behaviour, or the actions, of the men with whom the salesman deals. The salesman must discover what interests of his prospective customers are concerned with what he intends to sell. What needs is it fitted to satisfy? What qualities of the thing to be sold fit it to satisfy these needs or interests?

The salesman must secure the attention of the man to whom he wishes to sell. By presenting suitable selling points, in the form of arguments or suggestions, the salesman must influence the mental processes of his customer so that he arouses a desire for the article and a conviction that the purchase should be made. He must not only see that the customer arrives at a favorable decision; he must also see that he definitely commits himself to the purchase.

Argument, suggestion, attention, interest, desire, conviction, and decision are mental processes. To clearly understand them one must study other mental processes such as habit, memory, association, and thinking.

It must now be clear that in the act of selling the salesman is dealing directly with mental processes. The science which gives an understanding of mental processes is psychology. The salesman needs to know psychology in order that he may intelligently undertake to influence the mental processes and, through them, the actions of men. The master of the art of selling is the master of men. The salesman needs to know psychology as a means to the intelligent direction of his own life.

The general principles of the art of selling will be developed in Part I. This discussion will enable one to see what psychological processes are involved in selling, and how they are to be dealt with by the salesman. Parts II and III will give a clear understanding of the psychological processes with which the salesman has to deal. By means of illustrative examples, it will be made clear how a knowledge of these psychological processes will help to make one proficient in understanding and applying the general principles of salesmanship developed in Part I. It is obvious that much light should be thrown on Part I by reading it again, after Parts II and III have been mastered.

PART I
MAKING THE SALE

PREPARATION OF THE SALESMAN AND OF THE SELLING PLAN

This book aims to develop the general principles which underlie the art of selling. Special study is required to apply these principles in any special line of selling. Skill in the practice of the art must come from special study and carefully and intelligently directed practice.

The things one must do, in order to prepare to sell some particular thing, will vary considerably with the thing.

A detailed discussion of them would hardly be in order in a book which undertakes merely to develop and illustrate the practical application of psychological principles. It would be excluded on the ground that a work on general principles must not confine itself too closely to any particular line of selling. One who understands the principles should be able, by putting forth the necessary effort, to apply them to any special line.

PARTS OF THE SELLING PROCESS

In the complete selling process there is first of all the pre-approach. In the pre-approach one studies

PREPARATION OF SALESMAN 17

the special needs and individual characteristics of his customer.

[In this discussion the term customer is used to denote the man to whom one is trying to sell. Strictly speaking, he may be no more than a prospective customer. Yet it is well to treat every man solicited as if he were a valued customer. The aim should not be merely to make a sale, but to make a customer. The sincere manifestation of this attitude has a suggestive force tending strongly toward making both the sale and the customer. The salesman, who has this attitude, will think of each man solicited as a customer. It will do no harm to call him so in our discussion.]

On the basis of the information gained, he formulates a proposition adapted to the customer's needs, and plans his approach and solicitation to close the circuit with the customer's interest. After this preparation has been made, the salesman undertakes the actual approach, in which he aims to secure attention to his proposition and an opportunity to present it.

If he is successful in his approach, he proceeds with the solicitation. During this solicitation he may display samples or make a demonstration of the article. The solicitation aims to stimulate desire for the article and to arouse an impulse to purchase it. As the salesman goes on with the solicitation he must dispose of any objections the customer may raise. He must skillfully diagnose the impression he is making on the customer's mind. He must feel out the customer to see when he has reached the proper time to attempt to close. When the time is ripe, he must undertake to bring about the performance of the particular acts which the customer must perform in order to close the sale.

PRE-APPROACH

In selling a low-priced specialty, or article of general demand there may be little opportunity, or little need for the pre-approach.

The nature of the pre-approach may be made clear by the methods worked out for selling National Cash Registers. This pre-approach is divided into two processes, the investigation and the preparation.

The salesman is first instructed to make a note of things favorable to the success of the prospect's business. Among them are good goods, proper lighting, efficient clerks, desirable class of customers, etc.

The salesman should next investigate the method of doing business. He should find out the ways in which losses may occur. He may do this by observation, by conversation with the clerks, or even with the proprietor. To get the desired information from the proprietor it may be necessary to convince him of the importance of discussing his business with the salesman. In exceptional cases, by making a purchase, the salesman may secure information of much importance, which he could not get otherwise.

The investigation aims to give the salesman facts which will enable him to interest the merchant and show him why he can not afford to be without an up-to-date National Cash Register.

If the store is small, the preparation can be made

mentally, while the salesman is investigating. The investigation, the preparation, and the approach can all be made at the same visit.

If the store is large, the salesman should leave the store after his investigation and prepare a written analysis. For the largest stores this written analysis may be included in a written proposition. This proposition will give an explanation of the system proposed for installation, the location of the registers, etc.

The written analysis should list the good things found in the merchant's place of business. If the salesman unwittingly makes it appear to the merchant that he can see only bad things in the place and method of business, he puts the merchant in an antagonistic frame of mind. By recognizing and presenting the factors favorable to the success of the business, the salesman creates in the customer's mind an attitude which predisposes him to consider favorably the proposition presented to him.

The analysis should point out clearly how the system in use may be improved. It should show how the merchant lacks protection in the handling of his money, how he lacks sufficient information about his money, and why slow service exists.

The analysis should also give the cost of the proposed system. It may be well to compare the price with the cost of the system in use, or of some other system under consideration for adoption.

The written analysis, or proposition, may be used

in approaching the merchant to secure an appointment for a demonstration of the register. It should be thoroughly explained, and then turned over to the merchant and left with him.

The aim in the pre-approach is to enable the salesman to determine on a proposition, and formulate a plan of approach and solicitation. It enables him to present a proposition of such a sort, and in such a way, that the serviceability of what he proposes to sell will close the circuit with the customer's interest and needs. One can do this only as he understands the likes and dislikes of the customer, his point of view, his aims and ambitions, his financial resourses, the requirements of his business, etc.

With such information at his command, the salesman may make the aim of his appeal as definite as that of a rifleman shooting at a mark. Without such preparation the salesman must feel out the man he is soliciting by presenting more or less aimlessly a number of propositions and noting how they are received. His actions may be compared to a man shooting in the dark with a blunderbuss. With such a weapon it is more or less a matter of chance if any one of the missiles hits a vital point. When the projectile does strike the mark, it does not have much force, or penetration, or effectiveness.

The blunderbuss salesman reveals the fact that he is not master of his business. His random efforts make a bad impression which it is difficult to overcome.

Various firms employ persons other than salesmen to make the investigation of the pre-approach. The New York Edison Company does so in planning to sell its service to displace that of private plants. A technically trained engineer makes a study of the plant to be displaced, as a basis for showing the advantage of using the central service. The data he gathers is then turned over to the salesman, who prepares it for use in the approach and solicitation. This plan is adopted because the engineer, as a result of his technical training, can do the investigating more efficiently than the salesman. The salesman can make better use of the engineer's data in the actual work of selling.

Some firms employ men, who work more cheaply than the expert salesman, to make the preliminary investigation, and locate prospects with whom it is desirable for the salesman to spend his time, and to furnish him with data to use in planning his proposition, approach, and appropriate solicitation. The problem as to whether the salesman, or some one else, is to make the pre-approach is a problem of marketing rather than of the psychology of salesmanship.

The pre-approach aims to adapt the general proposition to the needs and characteristics of the individual customer. It endeavors to gather data which will enable the salesman to formulate a proposition which will meet the real needs of the man to whom it is to be presented. It enables him to plan intelligently how to close the circuit with the customer's interests.

Sometimes an effort is made to prepare the man to be solicited, so that he will be favorably disposed toward the proposition of the salesman. Advertisements in periodicals, and papers, circulars, and letters can thus be used to pave the way for the approach and solicitation. The general principles of advertising and salesmanship must be employed in such an endeavor.

APPROACH AND SECURING ATTENTION

In his approach, the salesman aims to secure an opportunity to present his selling proposition to a prospective customer.

A correct approach means more than merely inducing a man to notice that you wish to sell him something. It involves getting him to lay aside other matters with which he may be occupied and to concentrate his thoughts on the proposition.

The approach is greatly facilitated by a prosperous appearance, attractive personality, pleasant voice, and courteous manners. What the salesman says and does should suggest that he has a forceful character, ability, assured and important position in the business world, geniality, humor, etc. His tactics should be based on a general understanding of human nature, and such knowledge of the customer as he could secure from others, or acquire by direct observation.

Every one is inclined to be inspired by a man who knows his proposition thoroughly, believes in it enthusiastically, and earnestly wishes others to know about it and to be benefited by it. If a salesman meets these requirements, he will have little difficulty in securing and holding the attention of men with whom it is worth while to spend his time.

APPROACH

Let us first consider the wrong way of going about it. Do not ask attention, as a favor, or say that you would like to secure attention for a little while. Never say "I wish to interest you in my proposition." Whenever the words "my proposition" are used they suggest that the salesman wishes to secure the attention for his own benefit. The salesman always should suggest that he is endeavoring to render a service to the customer. He will do this by manifesting a sincere belief in the serviceability of what he is endeavoring to sell.

Do not ask for attention. Attract it. Attention must not be attracted to the salesman, or by the salesman. Attention must be attracted to the selling proposition and by the selling proposition, if it is secured effectively. If the salesman can secure attention to a request for attention, he can secure attention to a statement or question about the proposition, aimed to arouse interest.

In dealing with business men, the salesman should never resort to cheap trickery indulged in by some canvassers, in order to gain admission to houses.

The introductory statement of the approach should be worked out as carefully as the heading of an advertisement. It performs a very similar function to that of the heading. It should make some statement about the proposition which will arouse interest in it and make it seem important enough to demand a thorough investigation. The best way to arouse interest in a proposition is to state definitely and clearly, but briefly, in what way the acceptance of the proposition will be of advantage to the customer. Awaken a foretaste of the satisfaction he will secure by making the purchase. Put the emphasis on the service the article will render. If necessary, support this with brief arguments or illustrations making clear the importance of the service. Show why he can not afford to refuse to investigate. Keep in your customer's mind what your proposition will contribute to the realization of his interests, if you can make your claims good. You can thus get him interested in seeing how and why the thing will do what you claim for it. A good approach will pass over naturally, and almost imperceptibly, into the solicitation.

If the salesman represents a business noted for the excellence of its products or merchandise, and for the efficiency of its selling force, he may attach some of this valuable prestige to himself, by bringing out clearly in introducing himself, that he is a representative of that business.

In his approach, a salesman of investment securities could well put emphasis on the large and certain dividends, the safety and convertibility of the investment, etc. The salesman of merchandise could dwell on the timeliness, style, quality, and price, which will make them sell rapidly and bring in large profit. The certainty of good business conditions in the near future will predispose a man to consider buying. When interest is aroused, the salesman should then present an article which he believes of-

APPROACH 27

fers a very attractive bargain, and proceed to make clear its attractive features.

If the conditions of selling are such that it is necessary to make an appointment to go with the man to some other place to see samples, or the demonstration of the article, it may be well for the salesman to be on hand at the appointed time to accompany him.

If a man meets the approach with the statement that he does not need the article, have ready an argument to show why he should reserve his decision until after he has investigated. If he says he is not interested, make it clear that you do not expect him to be interested until he appreciates the service the proposition will render him. The plea may be that he has no time to look into the matter. Remind him that the salesman's time is valuable to himself and his firm. The salesman could not afford to take time to talk to him unless he felt certain he had a proposition that would appeal to him as a business man.

If the customer is ill-natured, or in an antagonistic mood, make him forget it by talking about some subject he is interested in, outside your line of business. If you can not succeed in this arrange to call again.

Approach a man, if possible, when his energies are fresh, and his mind is free. If he is so occupied that he can not give you his full attention, make an appointment for a more favorable time.

The approach should arouse interest in the proposition. If it fails to do this, the chance to sell is probably lost. Hence, the strongest and most attractive reason why the article should be bought, is not too good to use in the approach. The most successful fisherman is the one who uses the bait which attracts the fish most strongly, and displays it most temptingly. So the most successful salesman will be the one who, in his approach, presents the strongest selling points, in the most alluring way.

The reason why an article should be purchased, which may be used most effectively in the approach, as a means of attracting attention to the proposition and arousing interest in it, will generally have somewhat the form or substance of the general conclusion in regard to the desirability of the article, which the solicitation aims to establish.

Arousing interest merely means connecting the proposition with an already existing interest. The salesman can connect his proposition with an interest the customer already has, by showing him how it will contribute to the satisfaction of his need or desire, along the line of this interest. The salesman thus takes advantage of a tendency to desire already existing and stimulates and awakens it.

The following is quoted from the instructions given to the salesmen of a company operating a chain of cigar stores. It makes clear the spirit of courtesy every salesman should manifest toward those with whom he deals. The salesman who handles his customer tactfully does much to create good will for the store:

APPROACH

"**Always**—if there is no rush of trade—greet the customer when he comes in with a 'Good morning!' or 'Good evening!' or 'What can I do for you?'—or use any other polite phrase to welcome him.

"Call the customer by name, if you know it. A stranger should be asked to call again. 'I hope to see you again, sir,' and 'Don't forget us another time,' are good phrases to use. If you say the right thing the customer will surely think of you the next time he is in your neighborhood.

"After handing the customer his purchase and his change, say: 'Thank you, sir'; or, 'Much obliged'; or, 'Many thanks, Mr. So-and-So.' Two or three words of this kind must be said to let him know you appreciate the value of his patronage. Under our rules the customer who doesn't get thanked is cheated. Our customers go out saying: 'Nice chap, that!' "

"Get to know your customers by name. There is no need to ask a man what his name is, as though you were a police justice. You can say, after he makes his purchase: 'I'm glad to see you like that cigar, Mr. ——. Pardon me; but I know your face well and I'd like to know your name.' Then the next time he calls your 'Good morning, Mr. So-and-So!' will be a real welcome.

"Show everything you have in stock and suit your words to your actions. Give the critical customer a fair chance to make a choice without making him think you know better than he does.

"No matter what happens, unless forcibly attacked never dispute with a customer. Let him talk as loud and as nastily as he likes. Keep your temper. Discuss the matter quietly. Swallow your anger. Cut out the rough stuff."

SOLICITATION

AIM OF THE SOLICITATION

To solicit means to seek earnestly with suggestions and arguments, with, or without, the assistance of a demonstration, to create a desire which will lead to the act of purchasing.

In the approach, the salesman has succeeded in attracting the attention of his customer to the proposition. He has made clear to the customer the service he proposes to render in satisfying his need or interest. He has aroused his interest by awakening in him a foretaste of the satisfaction to be secured by availing himself of the service.

The approach aims to create a desire for the service the thing will render. The solicitation aims to create desire for the thing, by creating the conviction or belief that it has qualities which make it a fit means of rendering the desired, satisfaction giving service.

The qualities which fit an object to render service are the characteristics, properties, or qualities, or features which give value to the object. What makes a thing serviceable we call, briefly, the value-giving qualities of the thing. They are the selling points of the thing.

The purpose of the demonstration, which will be discussed later, is to make clear why and how the value-giving qualities fit the thing to render a desired service. These value-giving qualities are the talking points of the solicitation. They should be clearly and simply explained.

The talking points should be presented in the order most effective from the logical and emotional points of view. They should be so arranged that each leads naturally to the next. As far as the reasoning will permit, the points should be made in the order of increasing importance, so that the strongest will come last. If the points can not thus be arranged strictly in the order of a climax, each should be given prominence and emphasis according to its importance.

Talk quality first and then price. Quality includes all the properties, characteristics, or features which give the article commercial value. Quality, embraces all that makes the article desirable in material, construction, and design.

When a man has been convinced of the desirability of the article, he can be led to see that the satisfaction to be gained is commensurate with the expenditure involved, and that the price is therefore reasonable. Hence, price is a secondary consideration. It should not be mentioned until the demonstration of quality is complete enough to make it appear that the price is reasonable.

No matter how high the price may seem, the salesman should be ready to show that it is really low in comparison with the service the goods will give. It is, perhaps, hardly necessary to state that when goods are being sold for resale, the service the purchaser is to derive, is not to be measured wholly by the margin of profit on each thing resold. The ease of selling made possible by an attractive appearance, or package, the qualities which tend to make a regular purchaser out of the casual buyer, and other things, add to serviceableness. Judged on the broad basis of serviceability an apparently high price may be lower than the smaller price of an inferior article.

If the price is asked before the salesman is ready to give it, he should say that he will come to that pretty soon. The price quoted will seem low, when the merit of the goods has been made clear.

The self-confidence of the salesman adds much to the effectiveness of the solicitation. He should appear confident of making the sale, but of course should avoid over-confidence, or presumptuousness.

The confidence which begets confidence in the customer, through suggestion, comes largely from an honest conviction that the sale will be of real service to the buyer, and from a consciousness of being fully prepared to grapple with the situation.

To avoid the embarrassment and fear of failure which destroys confidence, the salesman should have thoroughly mastered what he wishes to say and do in his solicitation. He can then concentrate his attention so completely on the things he is doing that there will be no place in his thoughts for paralyzing feelings of embarrassment, diffidence, doubt, or fear of failure.

It is folly to commit to memory a selling talk worked out by some one else, and to give it slavishly word for word. One is likely to give such a talk with much the effect of a little child saying his piece. A talk, so committed and used, is so stereotyped that it can not be adapted to the changing needs of the solicitation.

The selling talk, down to the smallest details of expression, should be carefully thought out in words. It may well be written out. Each argument used in making a point, or in meeting an objection, should be thoroughly mastered so that one will never be at a loss for what to say, or how to say it. To accomplish this do not depend on memorizing by rote.

Fix upon the germinal or central thought of each argument, from which you may think it out again, or redevelop it, when you wish to use it. This germinal thought, or central idea, will be the general topic of the selling point, or the answer to the objection. Express this general topic in the form of a suggestive phrase, or brief sentence, which will serve as a cue to recall the argument in detailed form when the circumstances are seen to demand its use. For example: this is the "prevents loss," or "reduces expenses" argument, or the answer to the "I want to look elsewhere" objection. If the carefully worked out details of the exposition, or argument, are thoroughly associated with the topic in the order in which they should be recalled, one will always have at his command, ready to use effectively, all that bears on the topic. When what is said springs from such preparation, it comes with all the adaptability, spontaneity, and stimulating effectiveness of extempore speech.

When the various selling points have been carefully worked out and tagged with appropriate cues, the cues should be firmly associated in memory in the order in which they are to be used. Make the association links established between the various cues, in order to recall them, intelligible or logical, when possible.

The salesman should have the part his selling point is fitted to perform in making the sale firmly associated with its cue of recall. He will then be able to perceive when the situation developed in the solicitation makes it desirable to use a certain argument or exposition and can readily recall it. He should have mastered it so thoroughly that he can give it without much demand on his attention.

While making the point thus mastered, he can think ahead and plan to meet any unforeseen circumstances, which may make it necessary to change his tactics. When such circumstances are encountered, if one is properly prepared, he will recognize their significance. This recognition will bring into the margin of consciousness the cue of the argument he has worked out to meet this situation.

The situation unexpectedly encountered may be one not fully prepared for in advance. In that case he may find several thoughts starting to develop in the fringe of his consciousness. From these he can select the one which seems best adapted to meet the situation. His many-sided preparation has given him resourcefulness.

STATING THE AIM IN TAKING UP A NEW POINT

The discussion of each new selling point taken up during the solicitation should begin with a statement of what is aimed at in developing the point. It is well to have in the customer's view from the first, the conclusion to be reached from the facts or value-giving qualities presented. A selling point may be regarded as a conclusion in regard to the value of a thing, to be established by reasoning from the value-giving qualities of the thing.

To prevent the customer's mind from wandering, the salesman should develop his subject in a natural and logical order, as rapidly as the full import of the points can be grasped. If the man's mind is not fully occupied in following the visual demonstration and verbal presentation, it may switch to some other line of thought. If the thoughts once get to running freely along some other line, the sale may be lost. At least some efforts have not been effective, and some of the work will have to be done over. Hence, to hold a man's attention, it is necessary to keep new aspects of the problem developing continually. During the solicitation the salesman should dominate the trend of his customer's thoughts.

The salesman should not permit himself to be drawn into conversation about irrelevant matters, while talking the sale. In such a discussion the effect of what has already been said will be lost. An

STATING THE AIM 37

antagonistic attitude may also be aroused. Conversation about general topics should be had before or afterwards, if at all.

PUTTING THE MAIN POINTS IN WRITING

If a selling talk is long and complex, it may be well to write down each important selling point in plain view of the customer, and then proceed to develop it. The customer then sees at the start the point which is aimed at. The writing, in plain view, enables him to keep the general aim in mind and to more fully appreciate the bearing of what is said, as the solicitation proceeds.

With many customers the appeal through the eye is stronger than the appeal through the ear. The impression made through two senses is stronger than if made through either alone.

The attention is instinctively directed to movement or action. The observer experiences a strong curiosity to see what will be written. This impresses the writing clearly on the mind.

The points thus written down have a long time in which to impress themselves on the mind. They may be given additional emphasis by referring to them from time to time as the discussion proceeds. The written points will be convenient for making the final summary, when the time for closing is reached.

The customer feels different about a claim to serviceability when it is put down in "black and white". Such a claim can be verified. It must be fulfilled. It commits the salesman to make good in a very definite way. Oral statements are frequently discounted considerably. A written statement can be taken to mean just what it says. Making a permanent record of a claim to serviceability is an evidence of sincerity and good will. The service afforded will be compared with the claims. The claims must be truthful.

The salesman who uses this device combines the simple, condensed form in which the advertisement sets forth the selling points of the article, with the adaptability and warmth of a personal appeal charged with enthusiasm. The salesman should study the principles of advertising in order to use this device successfully.

ADAPTING THE SOLICITATION TO THE CUSTOMER'S MIND

The customer can assimilate, or properly appreciate the bearing or significance of what is said in the selling talk, only by relating it to kindred knowledge he has gained through education and experience. The salesman must present his subject from the customer's point of view, and build on the foundation of knowledge already present in his mind. However, he must proceed to elaborate, enrich and transform this knowledge.

The genius of the salesman is manifested largely in the certainty and readiness with which he hits on the right interest and ideas in his customer's experience to use as an assimilating notion, or apperceptive mass, to which he can effectively connect, by rational links, the points he wishes to make. He must make clear the relations existing between the customer's interests, experience and knowledge and the new matter he presents, pertaining to the thing he is selling.

The salesman's ability to transmit to his customer his own conviction and enthusiasm, depends on his skill in building up in the latter a state of mind similar to his own. To accomplish this, the salesman depends upon exposition, argument, demonstration, and suggestion. The ideas which the salesman presents tend to arouse in the customer's mind feelings similar to those which accompany them in his own mind. The enthusiasm and confidence manifested in the bearing, expression and talk of the salesman tend to arouse, through suggestion, a similar state in the mind of the man he is soliciting.

The salesman must not be contented with making mere general statements about his article. All such statements should be founded upon a broad basis of facts, or illustrative examples fitting in with the actual business experience and methods of the customer. A generalization is effective only when it is seen to be a conclusion drawn necessarily from an adequate foundation of facts. Such a generalization is full of significance and is dynamic.

EFFECTIVENESS CUMULATIVE

Thoughts, feelings, and volitions are controlled not merely by the idea in the focus of consciousness. All the elements in the dim background of consciousness, or that have been recently in consciousness, contribute their part in directing the mind's activities.

A well-developed solicitation sets to work a number of processes all directing their influence convergingly along one line, and all co-operating to bring about the desired act of closing. Each point made leaves behind it a trace of brain and mind activity, and a favorable emotional coloring. These persist as important factors determining largely the trend in the complex changing state of mind developing as a result of the selling talk.

Each point the salesman has made remains potent and effective while he is developing subsequent points. He thus builds up a constellation of mar ginal traces of previously made points, and of desire previously aroused. The effect of the appeal is cumulative. The persisting influence of the previous mental processes tends to fill the mind with a well-grounded belief that the purchase should be made. This influence also tends to prevent ideas of acting contrary to that belief from getting into the mind.

A properly worked-out selling talk can thus be

made cumulative in its effect. In a final skillfully arranged summary the salesman can stimulate to greater activity the persisting traces of previously made points, and direct their united force on the act of closing the sale.

In the act of closing, the customer's attention should be centered, not on the value-giving features, but on the act of closing. This will be developed more fully later on.

BRIEF SOLICITATION FIRST

In selling things which do not require a complicated demonstration or argument to make clear the service they offer it is well to make first a strong, but rather brief, presentation of the main selling points. Considerable material is held in reserve for future use, if the first attempt does not succeed. The first, determined, brief presentation may close the sale. In that case, to have used a longer talk might have lost it. At least, time and energy would have been wasted.

After making such a brief solicitation the salesman should sound his man to find whether he is ready to close. The methods of doing so will be discussed later. By thus feeling out the customer the salesman can find out what objections he will have to overcome. He will perceive along what line further appeal may be most effectively undertaken. He will discern whether he should aim to strengthen existing desire, or to awaken new desire, or whether effort should be concentrated mainly on showing that the thing is best fitted to satisfy existing desire, or that now is the time to get it, or that the purchase will not involve too great a sacrifice of other interests.

RENEWAL OF THE SOLICITATION

If the salesman's first brief attempt is not successful, he should return again to the solicitation, profiting by the enlightenment gained. If he has written down the main points of his preliminary solicitation he should see that they are kept clearly in mind. As he brings into play material previously held in reserve, he should indicate its bearing on the main argument previously presented. He should finally summarize his argument in a form more condensed than his first brief presentation.

Price should not be mentioned until near the close of the solicitation, as the customer may center his attention on price when the salesman wishes to direct it to quality.

Incongruous, irrelevant, or frivolous matter should not be injected into the selling talk. A pause to let a point soak in should not be long enough to allow the customer's mind to get running along another line of thought. Tactics should not be changed too abruptly.

If the solicitation is interrupted at any point, continuity is likely to be lacking when the solicitation is begun again. When the solicitation is resumed, the part gone over previously to the interruption should be reviewed briefly so that it will be present in mind in such form that the rest of the talk will connect with it properly.

TRUTH

To gain the greatest permanent success, a salesman should make it clear that his desire is to render such service to the purchaser that he will become a regular patron. The salesman selling to a merchant should know what style and quality of goods and what amount can be used most profitably by any particular customer and should give him the benefit of his knowledge. The seller should be fair, candid, and honest in his statements and honorable in his methods. He should guard carefully against making the impression that his chief concern is to make the sale, regardless of the interests of the purchaser.

A common practice among retail salesmen is to look closely for suggestions from the customer and to sell him whatever he may take a fancy to, even when he knows it would be better for him to buy another article. A better practice would be to give him honest and expert advice, so that his purchase would be permanently satisfactory. His good will and future patronage would thus be secured.

To illustrate this point, suppose a woman takes a fancy to goods that will fade in washing. If the salesman knows that a permanent color is required for the use to which she intends to put it, he should tell her that the color in question will fade. By so doing he **may** lose the sale. This would be better than to have the purchaser feel that the store **had** sold her a gold brick, and mistrust it in the future. It is better to lose a sale than to lose a customer, or to create ill will.*

It is wise to appeal to the good judgment and **intelligence** of the purchaser. Such an appeal is pleasing to the one to whom it is made. Every one believes he is intelligent, and has good judgment. He is flattered when others see it and admit it. Such recognition and admission establish a relation of equality and confidence between salesman and purchaser. Frequently the customer will feel that the reason presented must be a good one, though he can not fully comprehend the significance of it.

*See the discussion of "Good Will" in the author's "Psychology for Business Efficiency."

DEMONSTRATION

What one sees in an object is determined largely by the interests dominant in his mind, and by his preconceptions, or misconceptions. Experiment has shown that one may fail to see very important and significant features in plain view. He may distort what is seen, or believe he has seen what is not there. He may fail badly to apprehend the correlations and significance of the qualities of which he becomes aware.

In order that a customer may get the right understanding of a thing, his observations should be guided and directed by the salesman. The salesman must see that he brings the right ideas to bear in interpreting the observations made. The demonstration aims to accomplish these things.

The demonstration appeals to the strong instinctive interest in observing what others are doing, and to the instinctive curiosity to know the significance of it. Seeing a thing done is much more interesting and full of meaning than hearing someone tell how it is done. Doing it one's self arouses still greater interest in it.

In selling many articles, the demonstration is a very important part of the solicitation. Its purpose is to make clear what value-giving qualities the thing has, and to show how and why they give it value. It should be accompanied by a verbal exposition of the points of value in the thing and an explanation of the service they render. The solicitation supplements the demonstration with arguments and suggestions aimed to induce the customer to perform the acts necessary to secure the service.

The exposition aims to make one see the value-giving qualities of a thing, their functional interrelation, and how the customer's needs and interests are concerned with the service the thing is fitted to render.

In making the demonstration, one should not fall into the common error of assuming that because the customer's eye receives a retinal image of the thing, he therefore really sees how the qualities of the thing make it fitted to render service.

Seeing, in the sense in which the salesman wishes his customer to see the sample or article demonstrated, is a complex mental process. It involves a clear discrimination and a correct apprehension of the various value-giving qualities and their interrelations, and of the fitness of the thing as a whole to serve as a means of securing satisfaction. This can be accomplished only as the observations are properly guided or directed by the salesman. He must see that the right interest is aroused, and the right ideas are brought to bear in interpreting what is seen.

In making a demonstration, it is never safe to assume that any essential feature will be seen and rightly understood, merely because it is plainly in view. Neither is it safe to assume that the **significance** of a thing will be present effectively in mind, merely because it must have been apprehended previously. Familiarity breeds indifference. All essential features, no matter how familiar they are, must be pointed out clearly in the demonstration. Their significance should be brought vividly into consciousness. Many things do not become at all clear until they are presented visually.

In demonstrating a cash register the salesman is not content with pointing out that the indicator shows the amount of each purchase. He makes clear how the indicator gives publicity to the amount, and how publicity enforces honesty. He dwells strongly on how the total sales check up with the amount shown on the recorder, and how this reveals dishonesty or error. He also brings out many other serviceable features in a similar way.

AROUSING IRRELEVANT IMPULSES TO ADD FORCE TO THE DESIRE FOR THE SERVICE OFFERED

The salesman sometimes strengthens the impulse to buy by arousing irrelevant impulses to re-enforce it. The practice is generally questionable, and often deserves strong condemnation.

In olden times the auctioneer began by offering his article at a high price, which he gradually lowered until the sale was made. A similar device is sometimes employed in window displays, in which an article is offered at a price which is to be lowered a certain amount each day until the thing is sold.

In modern times the auctioneer agrees to accept a low price if he can not succeed in his endeavor to get a better offer. The modern practice is more successful than the ancient one, because it affords the auctioneer an opportunity to arouse a spirit of rivalry. He starts competition. He awakens the fighting spirit. A man who is bidding in competition with others may often be induced to pay considerably more than he would offer at private sale. The fact that some one has offered a certain price tends to make others believe that it is worth more than that price. In this way the desire to buy is re-enforced with impulses which could not be aroused by a mere

AROUSING IRRELEVANT IMPULSES 51

setting forth of the value-giving qualities of the article.

A salesman working for an unknown insurance company had to spend so much time and effort explaining about his company that his efforts devoted to the sale of insurance had but little effect. He had to sell the company before he could sell insurance. When confidence and good will for a line already exist, they strongly predispose one to respond favorably to the solicitation. Whatever creates good will for the business re-enforces the solicitation. See "Good Will" in "Psychology of Advertising."

ILLEGITIMATE MEANS

Some salesmen endeavor to gain the good will of their customers by entertaining them at dinners, or shows, or ball games, etc. Such means may predispose some men to buy. However, they are irrelevant to the end in view and their use is more than questionable. It is but a short step from such persuaders to open bribery which, of course, puts the salesman beyond the pale.

Some salesmen come to rely on making concessions to the buyer, rather than on forceful solicitation in which the value-giving qualities of the article are presented effectively. By so doing, they reveal a great weakness, either in themselves, or in the line they are selling.

MAKING SOLICITATION EFFECTIVE

The possession of a large, powerful body suggests that the man has corresponding strength of character and ability. Such a person towers above his fellow-men. They tend to look up to him, literally and figuratively. He has prestige because of his size.

A big man loses much of his size prestige, if a little man with whom he is dealing is placed above him. Regardless of the relative size of the men, the salesman loses prestige in dealing with a customer, if he sits or stands so that the customer looks down upon him. If the salesman can not be seated so that his eyes will be above, or at least on a level with, his customer's, he should stand.

The salesman should not lounge or slouch. He should sit or stand in an erect and alert attitude.

The salesman must be able to meet the gaze of his customer frankly and unwaveringly. A shifting gaze and embarrassed attitude are manifestations of self-distrust and self-submission in the salesman. They are a confession of weakness.

The salesman's gaze, expression, and bearing should show self-assertion and self-reliance springing from reasonable confidence in himself and in his proposition. The salesman's manifested confidence, enthusiasm, and mastery of the situation, tend strongly, through suggestion, to arouse confidence, enthusiasm, and self-subjection in the customer.

Selling is an important and serious business. The salesman should make his statements seriously and earnestly. His seriousness should not be grouchy or funereal. It should be good-humored and optimistic, but without the spirit of fun or levity.

The man who makes a serious statement and then giggles or laughs about it, destroys its effectiveness. Through suggestion he arouses an emotion in the mind of the customer which prevents him from taking the statement seriously and realizing its importance.

The salesman can get some hints for the effective presentation of his selling talk from manuals on public speaking and from teachers of the subject, and from studying good speakers to see what makes them effective.

Many factors contribute to effectiveness. Among them are clear perception of what one wishes to accomplish and an understanding of what ideas one should choose to accomplish it; the clear expression of these ideas in words and the arrangement of the words with due regard to logical sequence and emotional strength. Contributing to making these effective, are tone of voice, manner of speaking, gestures of head, hand, or body, expression of the face, attractive personality and the glow of honesty, earnestness, conviction, sympathy, confidence and enthusiasm manifesting itself by suggestion, in subtle ways, in the presentation of the selling talk.

The principles of argumentative exposition, of persuasion, and of rhetorical effectiveness, should be applied in arranging and presenting talking points. The persuasive presentation of the selling talk requires a personality and ability kindred to that of the successful orator or advocate. Knowing what to say and do is only half the battle. Half of its effectiveness depends on how it is said and done.

The salesman must secure conviction by well-reasoned proof, but he must not content himself with an unemotional assent to a chain of reasoning. He must arouse the feeling which will lead to action. The persuasiveness of his talk, as indicated before, will depend on what he says, on the logical and rhetorical effectiveness with which he says it, and on his personality and manner of delivery.

The salesman's argument is in the center of consciousness, but all the other factors previously mentioned help to build up around it, by suggestion, a fringe of emotional and impulsive elements which add greatly to its effectiveness, and prevent the occurrence of opposing ideas. Two salesmen may make pleas equally conclusive as far as their logical character is concerned. One may meet with mere intellectual assent. The other, through his emotional appeal, may arouse to decisive action. Hence, logical adequacy of subject matter must be supplemented by the other factors contributing to effectiveness.

We are not advocating overloaded attempts at fine

MAKING SOLICITATION EFFECTIVE 55

speaking. Buncombe, or frothy eloquence, will not fill the bill. What is needed is simple, **straightforward talk**, clearly expressed, and supercharged with the feeling which comes from the sincere and strong conviction of the salesman.

Business men are not carried away by mere **plausibility**. Build clearly the foundation of facts from which you wish your customer to draw his **inferences**. It is not sufficient to present good points. The solicitation must close the circuit of what is said with the interest already existing in the **customer's** mind. The proposition must be connected vitally and naturally with the experience and aims of the customer.

Secure emphasis by approaching the thing from a different viewpoint, and by expressing it differently, as well as by using strong words, or by repetition in the same words, or by emphatic delivery.

Strong speaking does not require big words. Big, strong ideas expressed in simple words and easily understood sentences are what is needed. Over 2000 years ago Tiberius Gracchus said: "The wild animals of Italy have their dens and lairs. The men who have fought for Italy have air and light, nothing more. They are called masters of the world, though they have not a clod of earth they can call their own." Men who can conceive and express strong appeals to interest in simple form like that do most to move the world. They move the world because they make a direct and easily comprehended appeal to the universal interests which grip the hearts of men.

Of course, when one is talking about a scientific subject to men of expert knowledge, he must use technical terms. Ordinary words are generally too vague, indefinite and ill defined in meaning, to meet the demands of exact explanation under such circumstances. Big words which express big ideas are all right in their place. Men versed in science are repelled by an attempt to express its ideas in the loose and poorly defined words of ordinary speech. Each new idea in science demands that a new technical term be coined for it, or that an old term be used in a new and definitely defined meaning.

Spencer sought to establish that "Evolution is the transition from an incoherent, indeterminate homogeneity to a coherent determinate heterogeneity, through a process of differentiation and integration." Some men have held this definition up to ridicule on account of its technical difficulties. But it set forth Spencer's idea in a form which was highly satisfactory to the class of readers to which it was addressed. Hence, it was used with appropriateness and good effect.

One should use technical terms when he wishes to sell scientific apparatus, or complicated machines to technically trained men. One should not hesitate to use scientific terms when addressing men well in-

MAKING SOLICITATION EFFECTIVE

formed on the subject. One should not be repelled by technical terms or treatment when he is trying to master the exact knowledge of a technical subject, such as psychology. Such a subject can be adequately presented only by using such terms.

The salesman should not present his selling talk in the form of a challenge for a debate. He should not argue with his prospect, or flatly contradict him. Avoid destroying confidence by too strong statements or by running down a competitor.

DIAGNOSIS

When a salesman is presenting a business proposition to a man, he tries to understand his thoughts, feelings, mental attitudes, and prejudices. He endeavors to estimate their influence as factors in determining whether the proposition will be accepted. He tries to diagnose the mental state of the man.

There is no science which will enable a salesman to predict how any particular man will think, feel, and act in regard to his proposition. Acquaintance with the individual, alone, will give that power. The minds of all men work according to the same laws. The salesman is interested in getting men to do certain things by influencing their minds. Through knowledge of psychological laws he will gain insight into their minds and skill in convincing and persuading them.

A knowledge of psychological laws will assist the salesman, as he proceeds, to estimate the effect his course is having. Such knowledge will help him to steer clear of obstacles, and to tell when he has worked his man up to such a point that he is warranted in pushing the matter to a definite conclusion. Knowledge of psychology, alone, will not enable a man to do this; such knowledge must be supplemented by a thorough understanding of many types of individual character.

DIAGNOSIS

Insight into the minds of men may be increased by studying sociology, political economy, political science, history, literature, etc., or by anything that increases one's general knowledge and culture. But skill in reading character and in correctly apprehending a customer's state of mind must come largely through a wide acquaintance and intimate association with men of all classes. One learns to deal with men through actual experience in dealing with them. A knowledge of the laws to which mental processes conform enables one to profit more by this experience. It enables him to perceive the significance of what he sees.

If one has the right sort of natural ability, a knowledge of psychological principles supplemented by wide experience with men, clarified through painstaking effort to rightly profit by it, may develop in him a judgment so accurate and prompt in sizing men up that it may be said to be intuitive. What is known by intuition is perceived directly and with certainty, without the necessity of going through long or complicated processes of thought. Such intuitive judgment is based on certain things actually observed in the expression, bearing, acts, or conversation of the person to whom it applies. We may not be able to tell clearly on what such judgment is based. Such is often the case when we say to ourselves, in regard to a man we have just met for the first time, this man is honest, selfish, or generous. Generally we would be very much at a loss if we attempted to justify to ourselves, or to others, such judgments in which we confidently believe.

When we thus say we like, or dislike, or suspect, or trust a person on first sight, or say that we believe he is stingy, or generous, or honest, or dishonest, or conceited, or stubborn, or what not, our judgment may be based on some undefined characteristic, observed, but not clearly discriminated, from the other elements of the general impression. We vaguely recognize a characteristic which has been an element in some personality which experience has shown to have the traits we attribue to the person now under consideration.

Just as doubt or conviction in your own mind will manifest itself in modifying your action, so will duplicity, knavery, uncertainty, desire, conviction, etc., manifest or express themselves unconsciously in the attitude, acts, countenance, or tone of voice of the person in whom they are found. Such expressions are the things on which our so-called intuitive judgments are based. Instinctive capacity and capability developed by experience are both factors which contribute to this ability.

Such judgment, based on what is observed in the ordinary ways of expression, must not be confused with telepathy, mind reading, or thought transference as it is variously called. It is generally agreed among psychologists that telepathic communication is an established fact. It is also agreed that it is so rare and undependable in its manifestations that it offers no help to the salesman.

It is not difficult to understand the parts of psychology with which the salesman is most concerned, the difficulty comes in making the principles practically helpful. When what has passed through the mind is reviewed it may be seen that the activities have conformed to psychological principles. We can generally say why any particular state has followed the previous state. Psychological hindsight is comparatively clear and certain, but psychological foresight is far less easy. For example, what is present in a man's mind will be followed by some idea previously associated with it, or resembling it; but this does not enable one to tell what particular associative connection or resemblance will prove effective in suggesting the idea which is to follow. Psychology gives the laws in accordance with which ideas, feelings and volitions occur in the mind, but does not enable one to foretell with certainty what particular mental states will occur.

Psychology teaches the "how" of the mind's working. It enables the salesman to do, with more or less certainty and assurance, what he would otherwise undertake blindly. Experience, guided by a knowledge of how the mind works and by an understanding of the principles of salesmanship, enables the salesman to undertake intelligently the task of starting with a given content in the mind of the customer, and influencing his thoughts and feelings in such a way that he is ready to close the deal.

The psychologist's attitude is abstract and analytical: the salesman's is concrete and practical. In a sense, the attitudes conflict and it is rather difficult to combine them successfully in one mind. Psychology is a science, salesmanship is an art. The relation of psychology to salesmanship is much closer, but it resembles somewhat the relation of biology and chemistry to medicine. It takes acumen, ingenuity, and practical ability to make original, successful applications of such fundamental sciences to the development of the art. But after the applications have once been made, many who could not have made them, may profit greatly by applying them in their practice.

Successful salesmanship will conform to the laws of psychology, whether the salesman has learned them from the study of the science at first hand, or from studying the applications of psychological principles made by others, or whether his observation and experience have brought him to conform to these laws without definitely formulating them. A knowledge of psychology should prove helpful in developing the best methods of salesmanship.

Since understanding the man as an individual is very important, the salesman will often secure helpful knowledge by trying before soliciting him, to find out in the pre-approach, something about his methods of doing business, his strong and weak points, and even his interests, outside his business lines. Frequently it will be impossible to get any helpful knowledge of this sort. The salesman must then depend on carefully observing the man while making his approach, and while soliciting **him**. Perhaps, if the man is not too pressed for time, he can engage him in conversation for a few moments, and feel him out in a general way before he gets down to business. He can thus combine the pre-approach with the approach.

The man to whom the selling appeal is made is generally on the defensive and tries to keep the salesman from perceiving what he really thinks and feels about the proposition. Since the salesman's efficiency will increase as his insight into the contents and workings of men's minds increases, he should avail himself of every resource that will be of assistance in penetrating this defense and discerning what is really taking place in the man's mind. He must not merely understand the laws in accordance with which the minds of men work, he must be able to comprehend the ideas, notions, interests, prejudices, likes, dislikes, beliefs and impulses of the customer as they manifest themselves in his mind during the solicitation. He must discern his customer's wants, what he knows, and does not know about the thing offered for sale, and how he can be most effectively influenced. Such are the things which will determine how the customer responds to what the salesman says and does.

The salesman must size up his man early in the

game and see clearly, and be guided by, the effect he is making. As the solicitation proceeds he must judge of the progress he is making by noticing carefully what the customer says, and does not say, his tone of voice, the expression of his eyes, and countenance, and his actions. Of course, the salesman can not be guided by what the customer says, unless he allows, or even encourages him to talk. Success in interpreting these manifestations depends not merely upon familiarity with psychological laws, but upon tact, intuition, insight, and ability to read individual character coming from a wide acquaintance and experience with men.

Ingenuity and resourcefulness, a forceful and pleasing personality, wise aggressiveness, and ability to inspire confidence in one's self and in what one is selling are essential to great success. The salesman should be a complete master of his line, not only in all its details, but in its general bearings as an economic force and in its relations to other affairs. When he is thus equipped and has the ability to diagnose the effect he is producing, he can select talking points adapted to the man with whom he is dealing, arrange them effectively and present them with telling force.

While proceeding with his selling talk the salesman may often find out what effect he is making by asking appropriate questions worded so as to suggest assent to them. Such questions are "Have I made clear to you the great advantage of this

DIAGNOSIS

feature?" "You see, now, don't you, why there is such a great demand for this article?" "If the matter is properly presented to him, it doesn't take a man long to see that this offers a rare opportunity for profit, does it?" "Isn't this a reasonable conclusion?" Such questions tend to secure assent to the cogency of the reasoning and the validity of the conclusion. By noting the answers to questions and noticing carefully the expression and general attitude of the man the salesman can tell whether he remains doubtful, or is being convinced.

It is often advisable, as explained previously, to make a brief, condensed appeal at first. After this the salesman can feel out his customer to see how the appeal has influenced him. He can then adapt the rest of his solicitation to the state of the customer's mind revealed by this diagnosis.

The salesman should study men as he reads about them, plays with them, talks with them and does business with them. Such study should enable him to put himself, in imagination, in the other man's position, and thus to understand him to judge whether the customer is in a state of indecision or whether confidence has been established; when to confine himself to straightforward matter of fact business talk, or when to use subtle suggestion or finesse, when to follow, and when to lead or use strenuous methods.

On the whole, sufficient uniformity prevails, amid the great diversity of individual character, that certain methods will work well with nearly every customer. In most cases it will be wise to stick to "the one best way" until good reasons are seen for adopting an unsual course.

As the salesman is presenting his selling points in his solicitation the prospect endeavors, from time to time, to consider them in comparison with ideas bearing on the subject coming into his mind through association; but he will not be able to do this very deliberately, if the salesman is presenting his selling argument effectively.

As the salesman makes each point and asks the man for his assent, he invites him to deliberately weigh the reasons for and against and to decide on the basis of the strength of evidence. When the salesman has finished his main demonstration and presentation and undertakes to close, the man will endeavor to balance the reasons why he should purchase presented by the salesman, against the objections or reasons why he should not, which have occurred to him in the course of the solicitation. If the salesman has not already discovered what these objections are, he should bring them out by appropriate questions.

DEALING WITH OBJECTIONS

When a salesman has succeeded in arousing a desire for an article, he is often prevented from closing the sale by an objection present in the customer's mind. Such objections are technically known in psychology as inhibiting ideas. As long as such ideas of considerable importance are even lurking in the margin of a man's consciousness he will not close the sale. Hence, objections are important things for the salesman to consider.

The salesman should know in advance what objections are likely to arise in the mind of the prospect. The selling talk should be carefully worked out in advance to take the wind from the sails of opposition by anticipating and forestalling such objections as completely as possible. But, no matter how carefully the salesman has planned his selling talk, he will meet with opposition. To overcome this, he should have worked over very carefully in advance the answers to all objections that are likely to arise.

The objections will vary according to the nature of the article which is being sold, and its relation to the needs, interests, and desires of the buyer. Just as it is important for the salesman to select the value-giving features or qualities of what he is selling, and to determine to what interests of the prospective buyer these qualities will afford a means of satisfaction, so it is equally important to find out what interests of the man are giving force to the ideas which serve as objections, and inhibit or keep him from buying.

Of course, the man may refuse to close merely because he is not yet convinced that the article offered is the best suited to satisfy the desire. He wishes to give further consideration to competing articles. The rivalry is simply between competing ways of accomplishing the same thing.

The rivalry may be between competing lines of satisfaction for the same interest. For example, if he buys an automobile as a means of satisfying his desire for recreation, he can not take a contemplated trip to Europe as a means of satisfying the same desire. Or, it may be that the satisfaction of the desire is not believed to be a matter of sufficient importance to offset the loss of the satisfaction of the other interests which must be sacrificed if the purchase is made. A competing interest gives force to the objection. For example, if I buy an automobile, I can not satisfy my home-owning interest, or my interest in accumulating money and being free from debt, or my interest in enlarging the scope of my business.

After the first brief presentation of the article, while the salesman is feeling out the customer, to see if he has reached the psychological moment for closing, the customer will probably avail himself of

DEALING WITH OBJECTIONS 69

the opportunity to offer such objections as have occurred to him. If he does not do so, the objections may be brought out by appropriate questions. An objection so raised gives the salesman insight into the prospect's attitude toward the proposition and affords an opportunity to connect the selling argument vitally with his trend of thought and feeling.

The salesman should not appear annoyed because the objection has been raised. He may say that he is glad he is dealing with a man who wishes to consider every side of the proposition, for it is one which appeals strongly to such a man. Let him feel that the objection is natural from his point of view, but proceed to change his point of view. However, show him that your point of view is right rather than that his is wrong. Never enter into a debate with the man or flatly contradict him, as you may arouse his combative spirit and make him feel that it is a point of honor with him not to yield.

In encouraging a man to argue, you bring into the focus of consciousness, ideas which suggest courses of action contrary to the one you wish to bring about. You start a line of thought which will allow all the interests you have created to die out. You are encouraging a man to try to think of every possible argument to support his point, when you should be trying to make him forget them. If the objection is the result of a misapprehension, remove the misunderstanding from which it arose.

When an objection is raised, face it fairly and

squarely. Answer it then and there if you can do so convincingly. An attempt to evade an objection, or a failure to meet it fairly may cause such action to be regarded as an evidence of weakness in the proposition, or a proof of incompetency in the salesman. If you can not fully answer the objection, say that you see clearly the point that has been raised. A great deal of its apparent weight will be removed by a clearer insight into the proposition. What little real force it has, is so far overbalanced by the advantages of the proposition that the objection raised will be seen to be a factor of very little importance. Minimize the importance of such an objection as fully as possible, and then rely on an effective presentation of the advantages of the article.

If much attention has been given to the consideration of the objection, it may be well to recall the advantages previously presented before proceeding with the selling talk. Perhaps a point of advantage can next be brought up which will greatly offset any force which may still be felt as inhering in the objection. It could be introduced with the remark, "Here is a very decided advantage which will appeal to you strongly along the line we have been discussing."

If the objection has been raised prematurely and can not be answered at that point it may be best to say "I believe you will find that matter satisfactorily disposed of when I have finished," and then

DEALING WITH OBJECTIONS 71

proceed with the solicitation, meeting the objection at the proper time.

What shall we do with an objection which we suspect of being present, although it has not been expressed? Even if one feels certain what the unexpressed objection is, he should not try to dispose of it by direct attack unless he is sure he can completely demolish it with unanswerable arguments. An unexpressed objection is probably lurking in the margin of consciousness. An unsuccessful attempt to answer it would merely bring it into the center of consciousness and thus greatly strengthen its force. Rather than attack an unexpressed objection which he can only half meet, one should depend on making his proposition so attractive that the customer's attention will be centered wholly on it, and the objection thus neglected will pass entirely out of mind.

Never suggest an objection for the purpose of refuting it, thus hoping to make your case stronger. One who does so may be suspected of setting up a man of straw merely to show how easily he can knock him down, or worse than that, to be endeavoring to distract attention from some real weakness in the proposition.

If the man will admit that the proposition is one that will bring him financial profit, but objects that he can not afford it, show him the loss of profit which will result from delay. Make him see that the article will begin paying for itself as soon as it is obtained. If you are selling him the satisfaction of some interest other than that of making money, impress on him strongly the satisfaction he will lose by postponing the purchase.

Suppose a man intends to buy, but that he does not close because he has made up his mind to investigate more fully, from fear that he may overlook a better bargain. Should one attack competitors, or try to show that their lines are inferior? An attack on a competitor or his line, might arouse suspicion that you feared to have the customer look around. This would increase his desire to do so. There is a motto which may throw light on the matter by approaching it from another point of view. It is "If your competitor talks about you put him on your pay roll. It doesn't matter what he says as long as he talks." When he talks unfavorably about you he suggests that your competition is affecting his business seriously. This suggests that one may do better by seeing such a competitor. People are likely to resent an attack which seems unprovoked and which is made under such circumstances that the one attacked has no opportunity to defend himself.

If you wish to explain the difference between your article and some other, you may say the competing article is inferior in appearance, usability, durability, etc., or you may say that your article excels in appearance, etc. The latter is better. Attract attention to the superior merits of your article

DEALING WITH OBJECTIONS

rather than the demerits of the other. When you meet competition, put your emphasis not on demolishing it, but on making clear the strength of your own claims.

If you attack the idea of looking elsewhere, you may merely bring it into the focus of consciousness and make it more effective in controlling action. It would be better to appear perfectly willing to have him make a thorough investigation. Express your confidence that no competitor can surpass your offering in real merit. Your bargain will appear more attractive after the other things are seen. It may be well to talk about something else for a little while. Then return to your article, paint it in attractive colors, make your enthusiasm about it and confidence in it so clear that you will inspire a like feeling in your customer. Make your proposition so attractive that it will fully occupy the focus of consciousness. Make the desire for it so strong that the inhibiting ideas will pass farther and farther into the margin of consciousness, until at last they fade from view and lose their force completely. You have then, in the terms of technical psychology, dissociated the idea of the act you wish to have performed from the idea of acting in a contrary line, which prevented or inhibited the performance of the desired act. Then is the time to make a suggestion directed toward closing the deal.

The most successful salesman is the one who presents his selling points or reason why, so skillfully, so enthusiastically, so convincingly that the attention is so fully occupied with them, that reasons why not do not come to mind. A salesman who consciously or unconsciously suggests objections is greatly increasing the difficulty of making the sale. It is often easier to anticipate or avoid suggesting opposing ideas than it is to deal with them after they occur.

MAKING KNOWN THE PRICE

If you succeed in arousing desire, you will no doubt lead the customer to ask the price. If he thinks it is too large, be prepared to show him it is reasonable; considering the satisfaction, saving or profit which will come from the article.

If he asks the price before you are ready to tell it, tell him you wish to make clear to him what it will do for him before you tell him what it will cost. Say you wish to make his understanding of the proposition so clear that he will be able to pass a correct judgment on the reasonableness of the price. If the customer is told the price prematurely he will be thinking about price when he should be thinking about quality.

FEELING OUT AND CLOSING

The fiat, or decision, or act of will performed by the customer in closing the sale consists in consciously dismissing or disregarding all ideas tending to oppose the deal, and in decisively accepting the proposition and giving the attention freely and fully to the performance of the act necessary to closing. Closing is cutting attention loose from opposing lines of action and centering it on the act of purchasing.

If the suggestive force of the solicitation has been strong, even if opposing ideas prevent the full performance of the act of closing, the act is at least incipiently performed. That is, faint tendencies to perform the act are manifested in the appropriate organs. These tendencies will at once pass out into the complete performance of the act, if the customer can be led to turn decisively away from further consideration of opposing ideas. The natural impulsive power of the idea of the action then becomes fully effective in bringing about the performance of the action.

To get the customer into a state of mind in which he is ready for closing, the salesman must keep his attention centered on the attractiveness of the bargain he offers, not on his own desire to sell. Every point he has scored in his solicitation, whether in creating confidence in the integrity of his firm, in the desirability of the service it has to offer, in his own knowledge, honesty, and judgment; or in making clear the quality, style, value, or other desirable features of what he has to offer, each point, if properly made, will have suggestive force persisting and converging toward the act of closing.

The sale may be lost by talking too long, as the salesman may thus suggest some idea which may again arouse a state of indecision in the mind of the customer who has practically decided to buy. The salesman must judge from the words, attitude, manner, and expression of the man, when it is best to endeavor to close.

The so-called psychological moment for closing is when the customer has become interested and convinced and feels a desire and impulse to purchase, then the time is ripe to make the attempt to close. To bring about this state of mind, the salesman, toward the close of his solicitation, should hold the attention of his customer centered on the most attractive features of his proposition, by enthusiastically presenting his strongest selling points in brief review, or summary form.

To determine whether the time is ripe to make an effort to close, the salesman must employ what we have called feeling-out suggestions. He may thus sound his customer by making a suggestion to action which, if carried out, implies willingness to make the purchase. Generally the suggestion is made by

FEELING OUT AND CLOSING 77

asking a question of such form that the customer shows willingness to close if he gives the suggested answer. Examples of feeling-out questions will be given later.

The suggestion that the customer definitely commit himself, gets its effectiveness, not through the force or persistency with which it is made, but as a result of the proposition commanding the interest and attention and arousing the desire so fully that it excludes all thoughts or tendencies to act in a contrary line. To prefer the proposition is to attend to it to the exclusion of other lines of action. To make the act of choice is to cut loose from opposing ideas and center the attention wholly on the thing chosen. When the attention thus centers itself on the act of purchasing, the recognition of the desirability of making the purchase becomes the fiat of the will that the thing be purchased. The customer then says the decisive word, writes his check, or signs his name, or does whatever else is required to close the deal.

When this stage in the solicitation has been reached the salesman should not ask "You don't want to buy this, do you?" or even "Will you buy this?" He should act as if he were reasonably certain he would do so. His tone of voice, words, manner of expression, and actions should all show that he is confident of making the sale. He should make his question serve as a suggestion that he buy. "This looks like a good proposition. How many will you need?" The salesman can handle the goods he is displaying, or his order book in such a way that he will make clear his belief that the sale is as good as made. But great tact is required not to offend the customer. It is only a short step from the attitude of the salesman confident for good and sufficient reasons, to that of the conceited and presumptuous fool.

If the salesman feels that the man is about to turn him down, he should lead him to talk about some unrelated matter he is interested in, such as baseball, the theater, church, or politics. When he feels that he has got him in a favorable state of mind, he should again present his subject with renewed enthusiasm and see if he can not carry the man along with him.

In feeling out a customer to find out whether the time is ripe to attempt to close, the salesman should ask him questions which will reveal the state of his desire in such form that the answer suggested would commit him to making the purchase. These questions should be framed so that they can not be answered by yes or no. Such questions are, "Which style, or finish, or model do you prefer?" "How much do you think you can use?" "How soon would you want it?" The insurance solicitor can say "When will it be most convenient for you to take the examination?"

The customer may ask from the salesman questions which would bring from him answers he

FEELING OUT AND CLOSING 79

should get from the customer. The situation may be handled in this way: If he asks the salesman which style or model he prefers, he can say "That is a matter of individual tastes and needs. Which do you think would best satisfy your needs?"

If the customer makes a selection, put it down at once. After you have closed the deal you can return to this point and rectify the mistake, if you think one has been made. Or you can rectify it then and there, but after it is down. Of course, the salesman should give the buyer the benefit of his wider experience and greater knowledge of the thing he is selling, and sell him what is best adapted to meet his needs, not what he may wrongly have taken a fancy to, through a mistake in judgment.

If the customer asks how soon he can get it, ask him how soon he will want it. If he says right away, say "All right, we'll wire the order right in and have it sent immediately by express." If he asks what terms he can secure, ask him what terms he would like. When he has indicated his preference, as to style, quantity, date of delivery, etc., put them down and say, "All right, sign right here, so that there can be no mistake about the details, and we'll have it here promptly."

In closing an insurance solicitation the following procedure might be followed: The agent could secure assent to his proposition by some such statement as the following, summarizing the main points of the appeal: "Mr. Blank, I am sure you will agree with me that every man ought to secure himself against business failure and provide for a comfortable old age. He ought to take every precaution to see that his family will be protected against hardship after his death. I have shown you an absolutely safe and sure means of accomplishing these things. I believe you see that the $5000.00 endowment policy I have explained to you will meet your demands satisfactorily. Your signature on this application (as he presents the blank and a pen for his signature) will insure this protection for yourself and your family. Be sure to write your middle name in full." The presentation of the blank and pen, and the remark about the middle name, center the attention on the act of closing. They suggest strongly that the act be performed.

If the man hesitates to sign, the agent should again summarize his main points, presenting them in his strongest way, and show him he is urging him to take a step in line with his dearest and most important interests. He should show that any sacrifice he may be called upon to make in buying this protection is so small that it may be disregarded in comparison with the satisfaction of knowing that his business is safeguarded, comfort is provided for old age, and those he holds dearest are protected against hardship.

In attempting to secure the signature the agent should place the order which he has made out as the

FEELING OUT AND CLOSING 81

points were agreed on, in a convenient position for signing, should indicate the place for the signature and offer the pen to the man as he says "Sign right here, please." If the man hesitates the agent should add, while still holding the pen and blank in such a way as to suggest signing, "We'll have it here on time and you will be even better pleased with it than you anticipate. You will look a long while before you find a better bargain than this." Of course, it is hardly necessary to say that the remarks given above can not be comitted mechanically and used in every case. We are trying by means of illustrations to suggest general principles which may be applied in ways adapted to varying circumstances.

The request for the signature must be made very tactfully to avoid giving offense. The customer will naturally resent very strongly anything that suggests that his word is not as good as his bond.

To avoid such an implication, as he places conveniently before the customer the order he has filled out and offers him the pen the salesman can say: "Please sign here to show that this order is correct," or "to O. K. it," or "to approve it," or "to authorize us to send it to you." On the order presented for signature the salesman should have written the "O. K." or "Approved," or "Authorized," so that the buyer can conveniently sign his name under it.

The retail clerk could attempt to close with his customer by asking "Which quality or pattern do you prefer?" "How much do you need?" "Will you have it sent out?" He could lead on a hesitating customer by such remarks as "You won't find a better bargain or a more becoming style than this." etc.

In attempting to close, take for granted, but not in a presumptuous or conceited way, that you have made the sale. The answers to the questions you ask, or the responses to the suggestions you make will guide you in further efforts to close.

Sometimes it is necessary to attack directly and overcome a determination to delay the decision until some future time. The salesman must show that the decision should be made now. The customer has all the evidence clearly in mind. He feels its full force. He is in a better position to decide now than he will be later on, when some of the important features will no longer be clearly grasped.

You have made a careful examination of this proposition. You are convinced that this article is all, or more than is claimed for it. You are conscious of a strong desire to secure it. You believe that purchasing this article will further your best interests on the whole and in the long run. Why should you delay. Your vision of your true interests is clearer now than it will be later on. Now is the accepted time. This opportunity is open to you.

The successful man is the one who has the strength of will, the decisive character, and courage of conviction which lead him to reach out and grasp the opportunity for profit when it is offered. By

FEELING OUT AND CLOSING

embracing this opportunity you will put yourself in a position to grasp other opportunities later on. In the past you have no doubt regretted that you did not inconvenience yourself a good deal to take advantage of opportunities offered, which your deliberate and better judgment told you would turn out well.

Your success has come from promptly taking up good things when they were offered. I am absolutely sure that this proposition is to your advantage --that it will do even more for you than I have claimed. My reason for insisting now is that I am more interested in your future success and good will, than in putting through this particular deal.

I would not be acting in accordance with the true interests and permanent prosperity of a valued customer if I did not urge you to grasp your opportunity when it is offered. Your interests are identical with my own interests and the interests of my firm. We wish you to build up your business so prosperously and to derive such satisfaction from selling our goods that you will be on the market for larger orders in the future.

Our future growth and prosperity is absolutely dependent on the increased business and profit of our customers. I am urging this matter on you so strongly because I know that here is offered to you a great opportunity, and I know that your acceptance of it will bring mutual and lasting satisfaction to both of us. Feeling as I do, I would be disloyal to your interests and those of my firm, if I did not urge you with every resource at my command to embrace this golden opportunity for profit. I am sure you will follow your own best judgment and grasp this opportunity leading straight to great and lasting success.

I recommend that you try about this amount. You will dispose of it so readily that you will want more in a short time. Shall we make the order for this amount? Of course, when the words "this amount" is used above, the salesman must state the quantity, amount, style, or type of article he honestly believes the man can handle successfully. The talk should be adapted, all the way along, to the thing offered for sale.

If the man objects that the amount mentioned is too large, show him that the experience of other men similarly situated has been that if only this amount is ordered, it will be necessary to reorder in a short time. If an advertising campaign is being carried on to assist in selling the article, show him that it is bound to create a large demand. Suggest to him ways in which he can display, or advertise the article so as to dispose of it profitably, etc.

If he objects that it costs too much, make clear the difference between an expense, which brings in no return, and an investment which will increase profit or reduce expense. If you are selling the satisfaction of some interest other than that in wealth, show that the satisfaction he will derive from

FEELING OUT AND CLOSING 85

the purchase will more than offset the sacrifice in purchasing it.

Suppose the man is satisfied with the line of goods, but will not close, though it seems probable that he will do so later on. The salesman could leave an order blank with him to use in sending in an order, though there was not great hope that he would use it without further solicitation. It will at least suggest strongly that he is desirous of getting the order and confident of securing it later on. The confidence as expressed may help hold him in line when he is approached by competitors.

The salesman can do something toward retaining the interest he has aroused, by asking him to remember that his goods have the quality which give satisfaction, and selling points which make them easy to sell. This is the line he will ultimately buy. Make it clear that you can give him pointers which will enable him to handle your line successfully. Get the advantages of dealing with you so firmly associated with the general line of goods that when he thinks of ordering in that line he will think of your line. Get his assurance that he will give you another chance before ordering.

AFTER CLOSING

When the sale has been closed, the best course for the salesman, as a general rule, is to let well enough alone.

In many cases the salesman's task is not ended when the sale is closed. Frequently the objections, or doubts, or inhibiting ideas which were lurking around unnoticed in the dim margin of consciousness, kept out of the center of consciousness by the effective solicitation of the salesman, will crowd triumphantly into the spotlight of consciousness as soon as the salesman has left. Fears and doubts and regrets will fill the purchaser's mind. Don't leave your customer in a doubtful, over-persuaded, or half-convinced state of mind, with a lurking fear of failure which will partially paralyze his efforts and make the transaction a bad one for him.

Leave the purchaser confident that he has made a good bargain. Give him suggestions as to how to make the most of it. His effectiveness in pushing your line will depend on his confidence in it. A hopeful outlook founded on a reasonable basis will make success practically certain. A few well-directed suggestions tending to start the customer's thoughts to working along the line of developing his proposition in the most effective way will help materially to keep the paralyzing devils of doubt from getting a prominent place on the mental stage. The salesman can thus pave the way for the success of his customer and for future sales for himself.

Just as the physician can contribute materially to the recovery of his patients through suggestion, so the salesman can use suggestion to improve the business of the customer after the sale is made. He can impress on the man who has bought, the qualities which give the article commercial value and the best ways of presenting them in selling talk, in display and in advertising, and the best way to handle sales. He can give him advice as to condition of markets, amount of stock to carry, coming fashions, and how to meet competing lines, etc. Of course, this helpfulness need not be restricted to the line the salesman handles.

THE DEPARTURE

After the solicitation has been finished the salesman should not make further demands on the customer's time. He should make his departure promptly and as tactfully as he made his approach. It may be well to express confidence that the satisfaction to be gained from the purchase will measure up fully to the anticipations aroused by the selling talk.

The salesman should thank his customer cordially, whether he has made a sale, or not. He should make it clear that he desires to be informed at any time when he can be of service, and say good day.

He should carefully avoid making the impression that his interest in the customer ended when the solicitation closed. The prompt departure should seem to come, not from a hurry to get away, but from a desire **not to** waste a busy man's time.

GENERAL CONSIDERATIONS

The true salesman loves the game of selling. He studies its theory and strategy. As the runner warms up to the race, so his enthusiasm increases as the competition becomes stronger. He is a good sportsman when he loses.

A growing salesman studies his successes and failures to find out why and how he made them. A man is stronger after each defeat, if he takes the pains to learn the cause of his failure and avoids that cause in the future. He is ever on the lookout for suggestions which will increase his power and skill. He finds them in the course of daily business, in swapping experiences with other salesmen, in attending conventions and in reading books and periodicals.

The salesman should acquire the habit of concentrating all his energies on what he is doing. However he should not hustle and bustle and waste his energy with unnecessary strenuosity. Over tension and anxiety are more exhausting than work. Worry and nervousness are great enemies of efficiency.

Every one should maintain a healthy interest in some avocation so that he can turn to it for rest and recreation. Some form of athletics, the theatre, some branch of study, any one of many things will do, provided he can arouse a healthy interest and forget business while engaging in it, and return to business later on refreshed and re-energized. One should eat rationally, secure plenty of sleep and exercise and see that he is fresh and vigorous when undertaking important tasks.

The salesman's usefulness to his firm is measured by his loyalty to it. He should regard its concerns as his own. He should not carry a side line which may lead him to neglect his employer's interests. If a man cannot be loyal to the firm which employs him and become thoroughly interested in his work, he should hunt another job. It will be best for both him and the firm in the end.

The salesman should have a broad and accurate fund of general knowledge, and be interested in the recreations and business pursuits of his customers so that he can talk interestingly on other subjects than shop. Ignorance revealed in any subject a well informed man should be up on, lessens esteem and destroys confidence. General knowledge and culture add to personal attractiveness and make not only a better salesman but a more useful citizen.

The salesman should ever try to excel his past performances. He should hold before himself a yearly, monthly, weekly and even daily amount or "quota" which he endeavors to attain or excel. He should keep himself keyed up to hard work. One rarely works up to the limit of his powers. He should cultivate the buoyant, persistent, resolute spirit which will not acknowledge rebuff or defeat, as long as there is a chance for success. When defeat comes, he should think of it only long enough to grasp its lesson, and should then devote his thoughts and energies wholly to planning and gaining future success.

SALESMANSHIP AS A PROFESSION

A study of the general conditions, factors, and processes involved in producing and marketing serviceable things is an economic rather than a psychological study. However, there are many problems in this field that can be solved only by the application of psychological knowledge.

Salesmanship plays the part of central and prime importance in the processes involved in the exchange of services or serviceable things. The function of salesmanship is to bring about a mutually advantageous exchange of services, or of serviceable things.

In order that the part which salesmanship plays in marketing services may be ranked as a profession, the salesman must attain a mastery of a fund of practical skill and special knowledge. This knowledge embraces the mastery of a body of scientifically developed and sytsematically organized general principles which must be applied in the intelligent practice of the art of selling. In order that the work of the salesman may be accorded professional standing, the special fund of knowledge and of skill in dealing with practical affairs must be employed in such a way that the exchanges of services which are brought about will be mutually and fairly advantageous to all parties concerned.

In order that the work of the salesman may be

SALESMANSHIP AS A PROFESSION

ranked as professional, he must have an understanding of the general and special problems of marketing commodities. Although a large part of this knowledge is economic, it may be well to take a brief glance at some of the more important features of the field. It may help the salesman to bear in mind that he should know and use more than is required merely to make a sale, if his vocation is to secure recognition as a profession.

PROBLEMS OF MARKETING COMMODITIES

A large problem can not be solved until it has been analyzed into its component parts. The general aim of business is to produce and exchange commodities fitted to satisfy the needs of men. To carry out this aim the needs must be clearly discerned and their importance for well-being must be appraised.

To realize its general aim, business must solve many difficult problems involved in the production and marketing of commodities. The solution of each problem in turn becomes a general aim which must be subdivided into many problems demanding solution. Each of these problems must also be looked upon as a combination of many problems. In discussing the process of thinking we have made clear the general method which must be followed in solving problems. We state here some of the problems marketing has to solve.

The salesman should understand the part his work plays in the complex processes of business. Business includes the industrial processes of producing goods fitted to satisfy needs, also finance, accounting, law, and marketing. The salesman performs a part of the work of marketing the service rendered by the business.

The general plan of marketing, or distribution, must be worked out by employing data gathered

MARKETING COMMODITIES 95

from a careful study of some or all of the following factors, according to the nature of the commodity.

The market must be analyzed. What are the qualities of the commodity which fit it to promote well-being? Is it demanded by all, or by certain classes? Is the consumption of it continual, occasional, or seasonal? Does it serve a permanent interest, or an interest which has the nature of a fashion, or fad, or fancy?

There must be a survey of the field in which the market must be sought, to find, among other things: the present number of the consumers of the commodity, their per capita consumption, and the prospect of increasing either this consumption, or the number of consumers; the ratio of present consumption to unit area of territory, in various parts of the field.

The production and marketing of competitors should be studied to determine: their number, their combined and individual output, the distribution of their outputs, their best and worst markets, the accessibility of their markets, the channels through which their output is distributed, whether through jobbers, or direct to dealers or consumers, by salesmen, or by mail order, their advertising methods, etc., the location of dealers and jobbers in the territory; the possibility of increasing the number, etc.

The manufacturing methods of competitors, the merits and demerits, and prices of their commodities must be considered.

Those who have the direction of the marketing

should know, the financial resources and capacity of their own plant, the cost of raw materials, of manufacturing, of overhead expenses, and of selling, the amount of business possible to be secured, and the amount likely to be gotten, the amount of business likely to be secured in various districts of the market, estimated according to the area and accessibility of the districts.

The one in charge of the marketing should know the cost of production, the lowest price which can be accepted, the best price which can probably be obtained, the amount which any possible lowering of price would increase the consumption, and affect competition. When he has determined the price which should be asked to secure a fair return for service rendered, he should be able to estimate the probable sales and profit, as a basis of determining how much should be spent for selling and advertising. These estimates should be based upon what competitors are doing, the comparative desirability of commodities, and, if the business is new, the greater cost of selling resulting from the lack of good will.

The plan for marketing must be adjusted to the various conditions of territory and competition. It must take into account the capabilities and limitations of its own industrial and financial resources. A general plan of distribution should be formulated which is adapted to all the requirements revealed by the survey and analysis of the market.

The general plan of marketing should formulate

plans for advertising and selling. The advertising and selling plans should be properly co-ordinated with each other, and adapted to cultivating the market most profitably. An efficient shipping department should be organized.

In developing material to be used in the appeal of the salesman, and of the advertisements, the commodity should be studied to determine, whether it has distinctive features of serviceability, or whether it is difficult to distinguish from other similar things. The name, the package, and the trademark should be carefully scrutinized. They should be made attractive and distinctive, and should be protected as fully as possible.

The articles of competitors should be studied to get knowledge like the foregoing in regard to them. The strong and weak points in their appeals should be noticed, and how much they have influenced consumption. The efficiency of the advertising methods should be noticed, also the value placed on various media as evidenced by their use.

The stationery should be attractive. Follow-up methods and material should be carefully worked out.

The salesman should have a sound grasp of the fundamental principles of marketing. He should master the special marketing problems of his own line, as well as the theory and practice of selling. Specialization in selling narrows the view, unless it is accompanied with progress in general knowledge.

The narrow specialist in selling can not view the significance of his work in the right perspective. He can not readily adapt himself to the changes in conditions that are certain to come. He has small chance for promotion to a position of greater responsibility. Every salesman should have a knowledge of the broader problems of marketing, as well as a knowledge of the processes of selling, and skill in practicing the salesman's art.

The salesman should be thoroughly familiar with the plan adopted for marketing his commodity. He should understand the general advertising policy, and should keep in touch with the things done in carrying out that policy. He should carefully coordinate his efforts at selling with the advertising campaign, so that the salesmanship and the advertising will be mutually helpful. He should also see that the efforts of the local dealers are properly adjusted to profit by the work of the advertising department. He should be a competent adviser in regard to their methods of display, their local advertising, etc.

He must know the previous successes of the house in his territory, how much opportunity there is for growth, and where his efforts will be likely to bring the best results.

The salesman should know the terms of sale, the credit rating of those to whom he wishes to sell, and the normal requirements of their business in his line.

The salesman should keep the firm informed in

MARKETING COMMODITIES

regard to the financial standing and business success of actual and prospective customers. He should be keenly alive to the amount and character of competition, its points of strength, and of weakness. He must know the style and quality of goods desired. He is ever alert to find how his own line may be better adapted to satisfy the needs of the consumers. The salesman must improve every opportunity to gather data which will be helpful to the manufacturing and marketing departments.

The foregoing should be taken as illustrative rather than literally prescriptive. It should be adapted to the particular conditions of the commodity. The aim has been to make clear that a man must be more than a narrow specialist in the art of selling, if he is to perform efficiently the duties of a salesman.

The aim of the business should be to render normal service to the consumer. The return secured should be only a fair exchange for service rendered. The salesman should be animated by the same ideal.

The salesman should be more than a mere expert in the art of selling. But general capacity and proficiency are not enough. He must understand the general principles of the processes of selling and have skill in practicing the art.

Psychological processes are the most important factors with which the salesman has to deal. The salesman must employ his own mental processes, so that he will be most efficient in influencing the mental processes of prospective purchasers, in such a way that they will desire and buy. To do this, he should understand the mental processes of his own and the buyer's mind.

Practice guided, not by general principles, but by haphazard trial, may give a certain skill. One may, in this way, attain to a certain degree of success without being efficient.

An exhorbitant price is paid for skill acquired by this wasteful method. The skill so acquired is not adaptable to changing conditions, except by the same wasteful process of random trial and error and the selection of lucky hits.

The salesman must not merely understand the general principles of the selling appeal and the function of its various parts. He must acquire proficiency in practicing the art of selling.

The salesman must know many things about the particular commodity he is engaged in selling. He should know something of the materials and the process of manufacturing. He can then give the buyer an idea of the materials, and labor, and machinery required to make the commodity. He should thoroughly understand the serviceability of his goods. He should know the serviceability of his line in comparison with competing lines; the points of relative advantage and disadvantage, etc.

By this time, it should have been made clear to the salesman that, in practicing his art, he is dealing with psychological processes. Attention, interest, desire, suggestion, impulse to action, and many others, have been dealt with frequently in developing the general theory of salesmanship. An attempt will now be made, in Parts II and III, to give a clearer understanding of these processes.

PART II

PROCESSES OF THINKING, FEELING, AND ACTING

BEHAVIOUR

Behaviour is purposive activity, or activity which aims at some desired end. Behaviour is intelligent, rather than merely impulsive, when it involves comparison of means available for the attainment of an end, and the selection of the means which the comparison shows to be best fitted for the attainment. Psychology deals with the constitution and processes of the mind as factors in behaviour.

DISTINCTION BETWEEN MENTAL AND PHYSICAL PROCESSES

Think about your brain! The brain is a material object. It can be weighed in ounces and measured in cubic inches. It fills a definite amount of space in the skull. Another material object can not be put in the space occupied by the brain without injuring and displacing it. When the skull is opened, the brain may be observed by a number of people at the same time. The brain is a manifestation of certain processes, known as vital and physical, the inner nature of which is clearly beyond our power of direct observation.

MENTAL AND PHYSICAL PROCESSES

Now think about the thing which thinks about the brain. This is the mind, or the processes manifested in the consciousness of the thinker. Conscious processes do not fill space or have weight. The head is no fuller and one is no heavier when he is thinking of a ton of coal than when he is not thinking at all. The mind is not in the brain as the seed is in the pumpkin.

Objects of the material world may be observed by many. As far as our observation reveals, they are not conscious of their existence or of what is happening to them. Mental processes are conscious of being mental processes. In the lowest, or least developed, forms of living things the consciousness must be extremely vague and diffused. It probably takes the form of a feebly felt striving. In man, with whose mental processes we are here concerned, the mind not only thinks, feels and wills, but also knows that it does so. In man, conscious processes are self conscious. In self consciousness the ability to observe and classify and understand the function of conscious processes has been developed.

SUBJECTIVE AND OBJECTIVE REALMS

The things, of which we have experience, but which exist independently of our experience of them, are called objects of experience. They make up what is known as the objective world. Our conscious processes which experience the external objects, together with our experience of these objects are said to be subjective. Our thought or idea of another person, or of a house, or other material object, is subjective, but the person or the house is objective.

METHOD OF GAINING PSYCHOLOGICAL KNOWLEDGE

The study of mental processes is carried on by introspection, which means looking within one's own mind. Every normal person can observe and describe, more or less satisfactorily, what is going on in his own mind. He does so, for example, when he says he is puzzled, or was imagining, or thinking, or feeling pleased, or angry, or striving, etc. The introspection which the psychologist employs is similar to this universally practiced self observation. The psychologist merely takes more pains to make his observations clear, accurate, and complete.

Progress in the knowledge of the workings of one's own mind would be very slow, if one had to rely solely on the results of his own introspection. In psychological literature, one finds accumulated the knowledge gained by the efforts of the best observers and thinkers of countless generations of men. Psychologists have gathered the general conclusions from this wide range of observation and experience, and have arranged and classified them and tested their truthfulness by applying them to experience to see whether they would work satisfactorily in giving us guidance in dealing with experience.

Reading, alone, will not make a good psychologist,

any more than it will a good physician. A book can only serve as a guide in pointing out what to look for, where to find it, and what its significance is. If one is to acquire useful psychological knowledge, he must become interested in, and skillful in observing what goes on in his own mind.

One has not mastered the general principles developed in this book well enough to make them helpful in the practice of salesmanship, until he can illustrate them with elements of his own experience, other than those given in this book. One has not mastered a thing until he can apply it successfully. Attempt at application is an efficient method of learning. One can thus tell whether he has grasped a thing. If one can not verify in his own experience the truthfulness of the general principles explained here and provide additional illustrations of them, he has not adequately grasped them.

EXPERIMENTAL PSYCHOLOGY

Certain mental processes have been studied experimentally. By using the apparatus and following the directions of the original experimenter, the processes can be reproduced as often as desired, under conditions which free them, to some extent, from confusing and distracting factors. In this way the conclusions of the experimenter may be studied by many different observers, and modified, or corrected, or verified as holding good for all minds. Experiment, when it can be applied, merely aids, rather than takes the place of introspection.

KNOWLEDGE OF THE MINDS OF OTHER

Psychology assumes that the minds of all men work according to the same laws, and that conscious processes and behaviour are similarly correlated in all persons. That is, the same conscious processes are manifested by the same forms of expression and behaviour.

Also simliar forms of expression and behaviour may be assumed to have resulted from similar conscious processes.

We can not directly observe what is going on in the mind of another. The mental processes of another can only be inferred from what he says and the expression of his countenance, and the tone and manner of saying it, and from what he does and his manner of doing it. These things that are significant expressions of the mental processes of others, can be interpreted rightly only as one, as the result of accurate introspection, has a correct knowledge of the processes in his own mind which have the forms of expression he observes in others.

Not only thoughts, but also feelings and volitions are communicable. Through understanding the interplay of processes in his own mind one gains insight into the interplay of processes in the minds of others.

In saying that we know the minds of others only

by inference, we do not mean that we must clearly discriminate the significant expressive elements in the total impression we are receiving, and center attention on them, and make explicit inferences from them. Through wide experience, carefully digested, we learn to apprehend the subtle expressions of the feelings and emotions of those with whom we deal, without being able, in many cases, to tell just how we do it. We learn to apprehend the symbols of these as readily as we learn to apprehend the thoughts expressed by verbal symbols. Our attention is not directed to the symbol in either case.

The ability to understand the feeling and motives of others is largely instinctive. One who did not have at least an innate capacity along this line that could be readily developed in experience would not get along well with his fellows.

CLASSIFICATION OF CONSCIOUS PROCESSES

Psychology aims to describe and classify the various conscious processes as they are manifested in experience, and to make clear their correlations with behaviour. As one observes his conscious processes he will distinguish in them three aspects, known as thinking, feeling, and willing.

The processes of knowing about things are studied in psychology under the headings, sensation, perception, conception, association, memory, apperception, judgment, and reasoning.

CLASSIFICATION OF CONSCIOUS PROCESSES 109

In sensation and perception we get a knowledge of our own bodies and of the external world. We may distinguish a mere sensation of warmth, cold, light, color, sound, touch, taste, smell, pressure, muscular strain or motion, without referring it to any particular object. But when we are aware of a warm object, or moving object, or colored object, we are said to have a perception of the object. We can distinguish a sensation of red, but we have a perception of a red apple. In the perception of the apple, along with the actually experienced sensation of redness, we attribute to it various qualities as roundness, smoothness, weight, taste, edibility, etc., which, our previous experience has taught us, are possessed by apples.

We form concepts or general ways of thinking and behaving in regard to objects, we pass judgment on them, and enter into extensive trains of reasoning about them.

We not only have various processes of knowing about objects; we are also affected by them. That is they arouse feelings of pleasure or pain and various emotions. A cut or bruise causes a feeling of pain. When you are cold, a fire gives a feeling of pleasure. Other experiences may give rise to the more abiding emotions of joy, sadness, pity, sympathy, hate, love, jealousy, respect, anger, fear, remorse, happiness, etc. These emotions spring from more complex intellectual processes than do the feelings. They are also tinged with pleasure or pain.

The volitional processes are attention and volition. They will be studied more fully later on.

The processes of thinking, feeling, and willing, are merely distinguishable, but not separable, aspects of the one conscious experience. Thinking, feeling, and willing are manifested, with varying degrees of prominence, in every conscious process.

MIND AND BRAIN

Mental processes are accompanied by and depend upon brain activity. Increased mental activity involves a similar increase of brain activity. The increased brain activity requires more nourishment and produces more waste matters to be eliminated. Other organs of the body such as those of digestion, the kidneys, the liver and the lungs must work harder to supply the energy and eliminate the waste. A sound mind requires the services of a sound body

Salesmanship makes heavy demands on both the mental and physical processes. The efficiency of the salesman will vary with the general condition of his body. He should be careful to take proper food, exercise, recreation, etc. Excessive exercise or severe manual labor impairs the efficiency of mental processes. Loss of sleep prevents proper nourishment and removal of waste matters. It causes a temporary loss of weight, with a corresponding decrease in the amount of energy available for work.

HABIT

When we first undertake to perform a new act which is complicated, or requires special skill, our efforts are hesitating. Awkward and groping movements that are bungling and ill suited to the purpose are mingled with those properly directed. We note with satisfaction the well directed movements, and endeavor to repeat them and to check the others. With practice, the movements gradually become better co-ordinated, more accurate, and easier to perform.

Painstaking effort, faithfully persisted in, develops skill. Finally, the whole complicated process is running smoothly. It runs along, almost without conscious supervision, while attention is directed to other things. Through discriminating practice and repetition, complicated acts come at last practically to repeat themselves, although they at first required careful thought and effort to perform them with indifferent success. To all intents and purposes the acts have become automatic. Acts which have thus, through practice, come to be practically automatic, are called habits. Thus we have learned to walk, to eat, to talk, to read and write, to sing, or play, or run a typewriter, or do the countless other familiar routine acts with which our lives are so largely filled.

The explanation of habit formation is largely physiological, rather than psychological. However, some hold that habit involves some psychical modification, as well as physical. The tissues of the brain are plastic. Plasticity means that the brain cells are modified by, and permanently retain, the effects of the activity which takes place in them. Nervous impulses, or currents of nerve activity, are aroused in the organs of sensation such as the eye, ear, or hand. They go through the brain, and then pass out

HABIT 113

through another set of nerves to control muscular activity. In so doing they leave an effect on the nerve cells, or a "path" that other impulses will tend to follow. By repetition, definite channels are developed, which currents of nerve activity habitually follow.

While these channels are being developed, conscious supervision, guidance, and effort are necessary in performing the acts. When the pathway of nervous discharge has been definitely established, the impulse follows it without guidance. The switches are set for the impulses in the nervous tissue to pass along the right tracks. The physiological organism has gained the ability to perform acts which originally required conscious supervision. It performs them more quickly, and more accurately and with less fatigue.

In forming habits, the brain has been moulded by practice. It has taken on stereotyped forms by means of which many of the routine acts of life may be economically performed. The lessons of experience are thus registered in habitual ways of thinking, feeling and acting about things. Familiar acts thus come practically to perform themselves, while the attention and intellect are left free to grapple with new problems and situations which arise. We thus see the importance of rendering habitual the routine acts of our daily life.

LAW OF ACQUIRING PROFICIENCY IN A NEW LINE

The movements, or procedure, involved in forming a new habit may be learned by the method of trial and error, or by imitation of others.

When the right procedure, or combination of movements, has been apprehended, the factors which make for success in forming the habit are:
1. Concentration of attention on the task.
2. Careful rehearsal, or repetition.
3. The avoidance of lapses into another procedure until the habit has been firmly established.

With the formation of the habit there develops a propensity to do the thing in the way being made habitual. The habitual way grows to be the pleasant way. A departure from it becomes unpleasant.

One should make a strong resolve to form the new habit. He should reinforce this by holding in mind the satisfactory consequences which will result from forming the new habit and the unsatisfactory consequences which will result from failure.

When a man takes up a new line of work, his general education and experience enable him to make rapid progress at first. Improvement is rapid at first, because the steps of progress are made largely by merely using old habits, and previously acquired skill and knowledge, and reorganizing them and adapting them to a new use. When these easy steps have been made, and when farther advance depends mainly on acquiring new knowledge and developing

ACQUIRING PROFICIENCY

new habits, progress becomes slow and difficult. The enthusiasm resulting from the novelty of the work fades away. For a time one seems to make no further advance in skill. He may even become less successful in the performance. He has reached what is known as a plateau in habit formation.

When a plateau of arrested progress or develpment has been reached, the faint hearted often become discouraged and quit. However, the knowledge that their experience is a normal one should give them resolution to keep on. When a plateau is reached, further progress depends mainly on the ability to hold one's self to the task by sheer force of will, until the new knowledge is assimilated, the new habits are formed, and the new skill is developed. Finally another stage of rapid progress will be entered upon, and may continue for some time, before another plateau is reached, and another stage of arrested progress must be worked through.

Our nervous tissues are plastic in youth, but become less easily moulded as we grow older. Under twenty is the time to fix right personal habits of eating, exercise, neatness in dress, well modulated speech, ease in intercourse with others, etc. Between twenty and thirty is the age best adapted to forming intellectual and professional habits.

To develop a new habit of this sort, start with determination and vigor to do the act. Improve every opportunity to practice it. Make no exception in favor of the old habit. One brief lapse into the old way, will sweep away much that has been gained by long and painstaking efforts, and will greatly increase the chance of future lapses occurring. Banish the old habit from your mind by keeping your thoughts fixed on the new one, and on the satisfaction to be gained from forming it. Keeping the old habit in mind develops an impulse to perform it which it requires effort to resist.

Every one should realize early in life that he must work out his own fate. Whether he is a failure or success depends largely on the habits he forms.

We easily become slaves to bad habits, or to poorly formed habits. The hell hereafter is not more to be dreaded than the hell we can make for ourselves on earth by developing wrong habits.

Habit gets one into a rut. We grow to like habitual ways of doing things. Constant self-criticism, alone, will tell one whether his ruts are carrying out of the line of progress and of greatest efficiency.

One should endeavor to discover the most efficient ways of doing the routine matters of his business and to make them habitual as soon as possible. Attention can then be centered on the important problems clamoring daily for solution.

The discussion of habit will be continued under the topic, "Developing Character and Personality."

ASSOCIATION OF PROCESSES OF THINKING, FEELING AND ACTING

The effect that the solicitation of the salesman has on the customer, depends on the processes of thinking, feeling, and acting, aroused in the customer by the suggestions and arguments used. The form which these processes will take depends upon the habits and associations previously formed by the customer.

ASSOCIATION BY CONTIGUITY

To make clear what is meant by association by contiguity, think of the word "stock" for a few moments, and then notice what thought follows it in your mind. The word stock may suggest to you the goods in a store, the paper representing a financial interest in some corporation, the raw materials from which something is to be manufactured, or a part of a gun, or a thing to wear around your neck, or the stock from which a cook makes soup.

A merchant would be most likely to think of the goods in a store, a broker of the stock certificate, a farmer of the animals, a haberdasher of the thing to wear round your neck, a cook of the soup stock. This is explained by the fact that each man has formed a habit of going in thought from the one idea to the other. When such an habitual process has been established between thoughts they are said to be associated by contiguity.

The law we are now considering is often called the law of association of ideas by contiguity. But in using the word idea, we should bear in mind that an idea is a process of thinking about a thing. Also that an idea may become associated with a feeling. For example, if one has become ill from eating an article of food which he has previously liked, the thought of eating the article thereafter may arouse in his mind a feeling of disgust, with its volitional tendency to avoid eating it. If a customer has been offended by a salesman, or even unjustly feels angry at him, or dislikes him for any reason whatever, the customer may thereafter feel ill will for the store which the salesman represents. On the other hand, a courteous efficient salesman, who is considerate of the real interests of the customer, will inspire a feeling of good will which will become associated with the thought of the business he represents.

The thought of the store is much more likely to revive the feeling of ill will or good will associated with it, than the presence of the feeling of ill will, or good will, in consciousness is likely to revive the thought of the store. We tend to pass more readily from the processes of thinking to the processes of feeling associated with them, than vice versa.

The following statement of the law of association by contiguity includes processes of feeling and willing as well as processes of thinking. If two processes have been in consciousness together or in immediate succession the reappearance of one of them will tend to recall the other.

ASSOCIATION BY SIMILARITY

If one disregards the spelling of the word "stock" and centers his attention wholly on its sound, it may suggest the word "stalk" having a similar pronunciation but a different meaning. This illustrates association by similarity. The law is as follows. A process of thinking tends to suggest similar processes of thinking. A process of feeling does not in the same way suggest similar processes of feeling. The process of feeling rather tends to bring it about that the process of thinking, or ideas associated with it, will suggest other ideas which have a tendency to arouse a similar process of feeling. This point will be made clearer later on, in discussing emotional congruity as a factor in association.

If you think of the moon, some idea previously thought of in connection with the moon may come into mind in accordance with the principle of contiguity. You may thus think of "green cheese," or of something you did on a moonlight night, or of something you know about the moon.

If you focus your attention on the brightness of the moon, you may next think of the sun, or of a light, or of some other bright object. If you focus your attention on the spherical shape of the moon, you may next think of a ball, or some other object of similar form. If you focus your attention on any aspect, quality, or characteristic of an object, the object may suggest any other object which has the same aspect, quality or characteristic, no matter how unlike the two objects may be in other respects.

Any object may suggest any other object which resembles it in any respect, provided the attention is focused on the quality in which the objects resemble each other. The similarity may be commonplace and evident, or far-fetched and fanciful, as in poetry. The similarity may be one of abstract relationship and difficult to perceive. A classical example of this is Newton's perception of the similarity in relations between an apple falling to the earth and the moon drawn continuously toward the earth, so that it moves around the earth, rather than passes off into space in a straight line; as it would do, if it were not attracted to the earth as the apple is. By assuming the force which holds the moon in its orbit to be the same as the force which causes the unsupported apple to fall toward the earth, Newton was able to demonstrate that the motions of all the bodies in the universe conformed to the law of gravitation. He proved the universality of the law of gravitation. The great inventor is the person who sees the similarity of relations which makes it possible to put a familiar contrivance, or process, to a new use.

The great poets and artists, and leaders in thought, the great inventors and captains of indus-

ASSOCIATION BY SIMILARITY

try, in short, the geniuses in every line, have minds unusually fertile in association by similarity. Fortunate is he who can see the resemblance of things!

An idea which a salesman presents in his solicitation may arouse in the mind of his customer, through association by contiguity, any idea which the customer has habitually thought of in connection with the presented idea. But other things being equal, the presented idea is more likely to suggest an idea which has been recently or vividly thought of in connection with it. Or the idea suggested by association may be similar to the idea presented, and will probably be in harmony with the existing emotional tone of the customer.

It is probable that the word stock, when previously thought of, revived the idea most firmly connected with it by habit. Now stock may suggest a neck piece, or soup, because the latter ideas have been recently in mind, and probably vividly so, since the association caught the attention because it seemed far-fetched.

If you were in a vindictive frame of mind the word stock might suggest the "stocks," a contrivance formerly used to punish criminals. To an unsuccessful or discouraged merchant, the word stock may suggest that he has too large a stock on hand already, and that he should reduce it rather than add to it. A successful and optimistic merchant tends to think of increasing his stock, as a means of increasing his profit. The trend of association is thus determined by the emotional state. The idea brought to mind by association will tend to be in harmony with the prevailing emotion.

His emotional state is an important factor in determining the thoughts and actions of a man. The "bull" is in an optimistic attitude of mind in regard to future prices, while the "bear" is pessimistic.

The salesman must endeavor to arouse in his customer's mind a general emotional attitude favorable to the acceptance of his proposition. He should aim to create a feeling of confidence that business will be prosperous in the immediate future. A desire for profit aroused will tend to make one buy the thing offered as a means of increasing profits. A vivid fear of loss will make it easier to sell fire insurance, or a fire-proof repository for business records.

MEMORY AND THE ART OF RECOLLECTING

The law of habit, manifested in forming associative connections among mental processes explains the ability to revive, recollect, or recall processes previously experienced.

The memory and recall of mental processes depends upon the fact that during the experiencing of the processes the structure of the brain is modified. A permanent change takes place in the structure of the cells of the brain and in the arrangement of the connections between them. The brain thus retains a trace of the mental process after it has passed out of consciousness. The activity has established a course through which the nervous excitation will tend to pass more readily in the future. A stimulus is more likely to follow a previously established course than to open a new one.

The existence of such an inactive brain path is retention. When the brain path is again stimulated to activity it gives rise to, or revives, the mental process which accompanied its formation. The process is thus remembered and recalled.

In studying memory and the art of recollecting, it is convenient to use the familiar term "ideas." However, we should bear in mind that an idea is a *process* of thinking. A process of thinking is found only as a part of a conscious process which also includes feeling and volition. The conscious process always has these three distinguishable, but not separable, aspects or factors, of thinking, feeling and willing. But, in order to get a clear understanding, it is necessary to study one aspect or factor at a time, while others are disregarded. In studying memory, our attention is thus mainly directed to the process of thinking.

When we are dealing with the conditions which account for the retention and recall of ideas, we naturally ask how can one increase his ability to retain and recall the things he wishes to know?

Ideas may be remembered and recalled as a result of associatively linking them together by mechanically repeating what we wish to recollect. Will practice in this form of memorizing increase our ability to memorize? Many experiments have shown that the retentive capacity of our brain tissue can not be noticeably increased by any effort of ours; though it will vary with our freshness, fatigue, health and age. It is possible to make great improvement in one's ability to memorize, but other methods than mere mechanical repetition are required in order to achieve the result.

The ability to retain and recall ideas can be increased only by forming improved habits of memorizing. The habits which make for efficiency in memorizing are a habit of clear and adequate observation and thinking, and a habit of discriminating and appropriate association. Both these habits in-

ART OF RECOLLECTING 125

volve the habit of concentrating the attention.

The prime essential of correct memorizing is to see that the things one wishes to be able to recollect are clearly and correctly perceived. The fact that one wishes to remember a thing shows that it has certain qualities which make it a factor bearing favorably, or unfavorbly, on the satisfaction of some interest.

The qualities which make the thing such a factor are the essential or significant qualities. In other words, the meaning of a thing is its bearing on the satisfaction of our interests.

The thing should be linked firmly by association with the interest whose satisfaction it concerns. The most salient, or characteristic qualities, that is the ones which will serve most readily and certainly as a means of recognizing the thing, must be singled out and carefully noted. They should be associated with the less obvious or significant qualities, or meaning, to serve as cues of recall.

We must carefully observe the essential or significant qualities of the thing. That is, we must note its bearing on the satisfaction of our interests. We must also note the significant and easily recognizable characteristics, and firmly associate them with the meaning of the thing. One should also observe the most natural or important connections between the object he wishes to remember and his previously existing store of ideas. These will be ideas closely connected by previously formed association with the interest concerned with recalling the thing. We must connect these ideas with the idea to be remembered by as many association links as will be likely to prove useful. To make the associative connections between the ideas as serviceable as possible, the attention should pass from one to the other in the order in which it will be useful to recall them.

Two orders of recall should be established. The interest should serve as a cue to recall the thing as a means of satisfying it. The thing should serve as a cue to recall or awaken the interest and suggest to it that here is a possible means for securing satisfaction. To insure this result one should notice these relations and should endeavor to establish firm associative connections in both orders of recall. The occurrence of the need should suggest the thing. When the thing is encountered, it should suggest an opportunity of satisfying the interest.

Suppose that while studying salesmanship you are looking around for an opportunity to advance at some future time your interests as a salesman. When you meet men who may be able to give you a position, or help you to get one, you should firmly associate the idea of the men with your interest in getting a position. Your interest in getting employment should suggest the idea of the man as a possible means of getting employment. A meeting with the man should suggest that here is a possible opportunity to get employment.

Let us consider a more concrete illustration. Suppose you meet a man and it occurs to you that "He may at some future time be on the market for what I am selling, or can give me valuable information or assistance." When you meet the man again you will wish to recognize him as a prospective customer, and call him by name. You will also wish to recall him when you are endeavoring to think of prospective customers to visit.

As you talk to the man, you should notice the most prominent characteristics of his appearance so as to impress a clear and accurate likeness of him on your memory. If you are a poor visualizer, and do not readily recall in memory, or picture to yourself how things looked when you actually saw them, it will be helpful to make to yourself a brief verbal description of the features of his general appearance which you believe will enable you to recognize the man when you see him again. You may compare and associate these with similar features of other men you know. For example, he looks like Smith but is taller. With this picture or idea of the man you must firmly associate his name, by thinking of it while making your observations. Use his name frequently while talking to him.

After the interview has ended, you should strengthen the association links you have established by recalling them and thinking them over. With them you can associate the man who introduced you, the place and circumstances of your meeting, the conversation you had with him, his business and social position and relation to other men you know, etc. Some, or all, of these, or similar associations you should form. You should firmly link them to your interest in the man as indicated above. Some men record in a note book the things they thus wish to recall.

If you wish at any time to recall the man's name, or appearance, or some fact about him, you can do so only by thinking over the ideas associated directly, or indirectly, with what you wish to recall, until one of them, or the combined force of all of them, suggests it.

ASSOCIATION PROCESSES IN EDUCATION

Education is the development of innate capacities of thinking, feeling and acting. Educational development takes the form of capabilities and habits of thinking, feeling and acting in such ways as will best contribute to the harmonious satisfaction of the various interests. This will be explained more fully later on.

The developed tendencies of thinking, feeling, and acting must be organized into serviceable association systems, if they are to serve effectively in securing satisfaction for the various interests.

PROCESS OF LEARNING

We may define the process of learning as the organizing of knowledge and skill so that they will be useful.

The efficient life is the well ordered purposive life. The efficient education is the one which arranges, systemizes, or organizes, the materials of knowledge and skill in such a way that they will serve most effectively as means of attaining life's purposes. Interests and purposes are the criteria by which one measures the value of things. Things have meaning and are valued, only as they are perceived as being in the relation of means to ends. The aims and purposes of life determine the selection of the elements to be associated and what associations shall be established between them.

Inefficient doing of a thing comes largely from inefficient thinking out of the method of doing it, or from failure to think at all. Efficient doing consists of selecting the essential factors from the unessential, and in skillfully organizing and employing them as a means of attaining the end in view.

In order to become generally efficient, one should formulate an ideal of efficiency and endeavor to attain it in every line of activity.

The principles of efficient learning and thinking

are the principles which make for efficiency in all lines of business activity.

Efficient thinking aims at the attainment of some end or purpose. Thinking will be discussed more fully later on. It deals with the solution of problems or the surmounting of difficulties hindering the attainment of ends. One must first think into his experience, or learn, what he would use later on in thinking out his problems.

When one encounters a problem, whether it is practical or theoretical, he can solve it only on condition that it suggests to him by the help of previously formed associations, the means required for its solution. The man who is efficient in grappling with problematic situations in an original way can do so only as his previously formed associations suggest original means.

The process of learning should be so ordered that it will be most helpful in thinking out problems. The most important question in education is how to organize the materials of experience into the most serviceable connections with each other.

One who wishes to accumulate a rich fund of experience, from which he can draw helpful suggestions when they are needed, should cultivate a questioning attitude of mind toward the matters with which his business is concerned. When he comes upon significant things, he should put them in his sinking fund of knowledge, by firmly associating them with the interests for which they have significance. He will then have a wide range of knowledge at his command, from which he can draw to meet the obligations of thinking, when they are encountered.

MEANING OR SIGNIFICANCE OF THINGS

The meaning or significance of a thing is the bearing it has on the satisfaction of our aims or interests. Meaning lies in the qualities of the thing which determine our behaviour toward it. Chair, as a general notion, is a symbol of a class of objects with which we may do certain desired things. We class as chairs all objects with which we may do these things. We pass judgment on a thing when we put it in a general class and attribute to it the qualities of the class. An apple has a different meaning or significance than a chair because it concerns the satisfaction of different interests. A bench has a meaning similar to a chair. But its meaning is different from that of a chair, to the extent that the bench has certain qualities which affect the satisfaction of our interests in a different way.

A thing thus has meaning only as it recalls, through association, the memory of previous experiences with the thing, or with a similar thing. Our previous experience with an apple has revealed to us that it has qaulities with which we are concerned in various ways. When an apple is perceived, the meaning attributed to it comes from the awakening of previously formed dispositions to think, and feel, and act in regard to it. A thing has significance only to the extent that present consciousness of it is supplemented by previous experience with it, recalled through association.

LEARNING AIMS TO GRASP THE SIGNIFICANCE OF THINGS

The purpose in learning is to discover the qualities of objects and the relations existing among them which affect our behaviour toward them, so that we can take intelligent advantage of the information in gaining satisfaction for the demands of our nature. We wish to know how our various interests will be affected by the various changes which may occur among the things of our experience. Knowledge aims at grasping the qualities and correlations of the objects of our experience so that we can deal with them intelligently in our efforts to secure the satisfaction of our interests.

Learning is a process of adjusting one's self to a new factor of experience, by the light of present and past experience, so that the factor will be properly appraised when it is again encountered in experience, or is considered as an element of future experience; and so, also, that the factor can be recalled when the needs of future experience so require.

The process of recognizing the signficant qualities and inter-relations of the various objects of experience is a process of judgment and inference.

MOST EFFICIENT METHOD OF LEARNING

To apply the most efficient method of learning, one should first find out the general nature and significance of the thing he is undertaking to learn. He should make a preliminary survey to see what interest is concerned with it, and the way it concerns the interest.

The next step is to get an adequate understanding of what is to be learned. The endeavor should be to get a clear, definite, and complete impression of all the parts of the thing in the order or arrangement in which they are presented.

In the third stage of learning, one should aim to select the more significant features, or qualities and characteristics, and to discern their relationships. Effort should be concentrated mainly on the proper understanding and arrangement of the more significant points. Less important matters should receive less attention.

In the last stage one should see that the general meaning, purpose, or bearing, of what is being learned is clearly in mind. He should review the associations fixed upon as most important, and see that they are properly organized and correlated with each other, in view of the general purpose.

By attentive and thoughtful repetition, the meaningful associations should then be firmly associated with each other, and with the general purpose, in the order in which it will be most advantageous to recall them. A written outline will often give valuable help to learning.

Learning should be undertaken as a process of organizing the materials of knowledge in such a way that they will be most serviceable in attaining the purposes one endeavors to realize. Associations of resemblance or contrast, or contiguity, or class and member of the class, cause and effect, etc., will have ultimate value only as they supply means for realizing the ends which our trains of thought are endeavoring to reach. Hence, we see the importance of keeping aims and purposes in mind while forming the associations.

If one is to gain the greatest profit from the reading he does, he should apply the right method of learning. He should endeavor to grasp and condense or summarize the significant points of what he reads. He should fix upon the general topics to serve as cues of recall. He should make similar summaries of the subordinate points to be recalled under each general topic. While establishing meaningful associations among minor topics, he should at the same time, keep the general topic, under which they come, in mind, and link them firmly to it by similar associations.

He should clearly perceive the relations of the general topics as parts of an organic whole, and firmly fix in memory the perceived relations.

Learning should always be a process of working over and reconstructing in terms of one's own thought processes. In this there should be a wise selection and emphasis of what is significant for the realization of one's purposes.

The reader should be able to reproduce in his own words the definitions, generalizations, deductions, and other thought connections occurring in what is read. He should be able to make a systematic recapitulation, or summary, of what has been read. Taking brief notes will often prove of great practical help in mastering what is read, so that one can reproduce, in logical continuity, its salient features when one needs to recall them in his thinking.

When one is endeavoring to learn so as to reproduce verbatim, he should endeavor in like manner to grasp and organize the features which give the thing significance. He can thus greatly lessen the effort required in memorizing and increase the practical value of what is learned.

The great disadvantage of learning by means of arbitrary mnemonic devices, such as are employed in many advertised systems of memory culture, results from the fact that one does not grasp the meaning of the material so learned. Hence, the material is not available as a means of attaining the purposes which determine the trend of our activites. Bonds of association that are not meaningful are generally of little practical value.

It is generally more advantageous to undertake to

learn as a whole than in parts. But if the amount to be learned is so large that it seems expedient to break it up into parts, each part should be attacked according to the method outlined above. The various parts should be finally joined and organized as a whole and firmly associated with each other. In order to link a following part with a preceding part, by means of a cue of recall with which it has been associated, the general bearing and cue of recall of the following part should be held in mind while the preceding part is being reviewed and firmly associated with the following part. This cue should be one from which the various points of the following part can be developed readily in the proper order.

As the last stage of learning, one should practice recall in reviewing the whole until it can be reproduced readily. Weak associations should be strengthened. The practice in recall should be carried considerably beyond a point at which the whole can first be correctly reproduced. While practicing reproduction, the speed of recall can be gradually increased. What has thus been learned should be carefully reviewed on succeeding days, until it can be reproduced correctly and without hesitation. One should improve the earliest possible opportunity to make the first recall of what he endeavors to learn.

If learning is to be carried on most effectively, the attention must be intensely concentrated on the thing to be learned. Such application is very tiring.

One should not continue his attempt at learning until the element of fatigue paralyzes his effort.

After an attempt at learning, one should let his mind rest for a few minutes before undertaking something else. During this time the associations are becoming fixed. Their formation would be interfered with if other things were actively taken up. A brief rest will prevent such interference, or **retroactive inhibition, as it** is called.

INTEREST AND ATTENTION

Every one knows, in a general way, what is meant by interest and attention. At times one attends closely to an event he is witnessing, or to a conversation or speech he is hearing, or to a proposition which is being presented to him. At other times his attention wanders. He accounts for his inattention by saying he is not interested in the thing. It gives or promises no pleasure. It does not concern his fortune or welfare. One is likely to be inattentive to what a person says, if his personality repels, or his approach is not tactful.

Inattention to a thing that becomes an element of consciousness results from the fact that the attention is given to some other thing which arouses more interest. Absent-mindedness is a state in which one's attention is so completely concentrated on developing one line of thought that he does not notice other things which otherwise might arouse interest.

We may get a clearer notion of the nature of interest, from which attention results, and its relation to objects, by considering concrete examples. Ordinarily one is not interested in a time table. Even if he notices it, he at once turns his attention to some other object. But if one is going to take a journey, he may become intensely interested in a time table as a means of learning the trains that will take him to his destination most conveniently. One's interest in the time table is satisfied, and his attention to it ends, when he has gained the desired information. His aim, or purpose, has been realized and his interest has been satisfied.

Perhaps the reader has previously had no interest in psychology, but has been led to believe that he can learn something from it which will enable him to improve his efficiency as a salesman. If he finds that an understanding of psychology will enable him to solve the problems of salesmanship more satisfactorily, he will become interested in psychology.

Objects not interesting in themselves will become so by bringing them into a significant relation to that which is already interesting. Show a man that the object you wish to sell him is the best means of realizing some aim or purpose he is interested in gaining and he will become interested in the object and will desire it.

At first one may be interested in **accumulating** money as a means of securing satisfaction for other interests. As one labors to **accumlate** wealth, his interest may be transferred from the things the wealth will secure and, through association, may become attached to and centered wholly on the accumulation of money as a means of securing satisfaction, as the traditional miser is attracted to and hoards his gold.

VOLUNTARY AND SPONTANEOUS ATTENTION

It is helpful to distinguish between voluntary and spontaneous attention.

Voluntary attention is attention directed to an object by an act of will, influenced by some motive other than interest in the thing attended to. A prospective customer may give this sort of willed attention to an article because of a request made by the salesman. Perhaps the salesman has assured him that the article will be a satisfactory means to the realization of some purpose in which he is interested. For example, the salesman may claim that the article will save expense and prevent losses. If the customer finds in the article nothing to warrant the salesman's assertion, he does not become interested in it and his attention soon wanders from it.

If the selling talk and demonstration of the salesman lead the man solicited to discover in the article a promise of bringing about the saving claimed for it, he will become interested in it and his attention will remain fixed upon it for some time. To hold the attention when it is once secured, the salesman must continue to develop interesting points, and thus lead the customer to discover in the object a growing promise of making the desired saving. This spontaneous, or nonvoluntary attention, held by the developing interest in the object, is what the salesman must secure, if he is to be successful.

Expectation of securing satisfaction arouses voluntary attention. Progressive satisfaction of the expectation leads to spontaneous attention.

That is attended to which seems to concern the satisfaction of the aims, purposes, interests, or instincts which at the time are more or less clearly in consciousness. Passive attention of an instinctive sort is given to intense, moving, pleasant, and unpleasant stimuli, to those which arouse curiosity and those which have a rhythmic character, etc. The various instincts and interests and their part in influencing conduct will be discussed later.

We give spontaneous attention to a thing we are conscious of being immediately concerned with. Such a thing takes on the aspect of being interesting in and of itself. It requires no effort to attend to such things.

Voluntary attention is given to a thing which is not in itself immediately interesting, but on the ground that it may concern, or is believed to concern, the future satisfaction of some interest. Such attention is very fatiguing. The ability to give attention of this sort, which is sustained for any considerable length of time, can be developed only by a rigorous course of training.

The power of giving sustained voluntary attention is the ability which enables one to direct his efforts persistently and unswervingly toward the attainment of some aim or ideal. The end to be gained is the motive which gives the trend to conscious activities.

VOLUNTARY AND SPONTANEOUS ATTENTION

Things thus attended to through voluntary attention tend to become immediately interesting. The interest is transferred to them through association. Henceforth they may arouse spontaneous attention.

Tasks which were at first uninteresting or positively disagreeable, may thus become interesting. The business man will finally come to turn with pleasure to tasks which originally aroused a feeling of repugnance. A knowledge of this fact may do much to encourage one to put forth the initial efforts required to perform certain unpleasant tasks connected with new work he is undertaking.

The idea of taking up a new task arouses a feeling of repugnance. The first efforts are put forth with reluctance. Persistence in the efforts tends gradually to overcome the antagonism felt for the task. The work done grows accordingly in efficiency. One should accustom himself to taking up new tasks that seem uninteresting with the consciousness that the worst will come first, and will soon be over. It is like a cold plunge. The first contact with the water is painful, but the final result is stimulating.

There is a rhythmic rise and fall in the effectiveness of attentive effort. As the power of attention wanes, the task may come to seem irksome. There is a tendency to yield to distracting influences. Under such circumstances, if one can hold himself resolutely to the task, he will find his efficiency again increasing with the rising wave of attention.

In order to accomplish things worth while, one

must be able to put forth a persistent effort to attain a remote end. He must have the ability to resist the distracting influences which tend to lure him aside. Such ability can come only through the formation of habit, as was previously explained.

FOCUS AND MARGIN OF ATTENTION

The focus of attention is the spot light on the stage of consciousness. When an idea is in the clear central light of consciousness it is said to be in the focus. Surrounding this center of clear perception are ideas of which we are but dimly and vaguely aware, if we are at all aware, that they are in consciousness. These are known as marginal ideas.

The reader can make clear to himself the distinction between the focus and margin, by practicing introspection. He will find that, as he reads, the focus is filled with what he is reading. There are, no doubt, ideas in the margin of his consciousness at the same time, which he can become conscious of, if he pauses to notice them. He may find among these ideas the ticking of a clock, the sound of people walking or talking in the house, the noises of the street, etc.

Ideas not attended to do not get into the clear center of consciousness, but remain obscurely in the margin, and soon drop out of mind.

The mind is focused on the idea to which it attends. Such an idea becomes clearer and remains longer in consciousness. Close attention to an idea makes it more likely to be remembered. By attending to an idea we bring it about that the ideas associated with it will come next into mind.

One can not give concentrated and effective attention to more than one thing at a time. However, one can get along fairly well in doing some task which he has made habitual or familiar through practice, and which as a result requires but little attentive effort, while, at the same time, his attention is focused on some unfamiliar, or difficult task which requires delicate adjustments to meet new conditions.

One can attend to an end to be gained and at the same time compare, criticise, choose, or use, means fitted to gain the end. But in any case when one attempts to attend to things which are not parts of one general process, or are not closely related to each other, the attention will alternate between them. Neither can get the effective attention which either alone would receive. Divided or distracted attention results in weak feeling, feeble impulses to action, and indecisive action.

EXPECTANT ATTENTION

Some of a magician's success comes from baffling the eye of the spectator. A greater part of it comes from diverting the attention from significant or essential things, and centering it, by suggestion, on features which do not reveal the true explanation.

The magician also creates a state of expectant attention. By carefully planned and skillfully employed suggestions, he works the spectator up into a sympathetic state of mind. He leads the onlooker to expect vividly that the result he proposes to attain will be secured by the means, or process, he pretends to use. Criticism has been forestalled by predisposing to belief that the result will come in the way and form specified by the wonder worker. This belief fills the mind of the onlooker so fully that he sees what he strongly believes he will see.

A preconception of the intellectual sort will warp observation and judgment. A practiced reader does not readily see misprints. He overlooks them easily, even when looking for them. One standing on a crowded street looking for a friend to come along, may believe he sees him many times before he really appears. He may mistake for his familiar friend, men who are very unlike him.

Expectant attention often leads one to misjudge the real qualities of objects presented for his consideration. One sees what he expects to see. If one approaches a proposition in a skeptical frame of mind, he finds things which arouse suspicion and exaggerates their importance. If one is confident that everything will turn out all right, he is less critical. We prejudge the article favorably. Our mind is colored by the satisfaction we expect to receive. In this state of mind we are likely to overlook weak points, and see only the good ones. Good will as a business asset is largely a predisposition to look for satisfaction.

A strong desire, mingling with a strong feeling of confidence, often leads one to act without giving due consideration to factors indicating the wisdom of another line of action. The fraudulent advertisement, or selling proposition, creates and takes advantage of such an uncritical state of mind. Attention is centered on some strong claim, or alluring promise. Desire is aroused. The mind is filled with a foretaste of the satisfaction which will result, if the attractive promise is made good. The person is made to believe that he is in danger of losing the golden opportunity, if he does not act at once. In such a state of mind, the weak features of the proposition do not receive proper consideration.

ATTENTION DETERMINES THE DIRECTION OF THINKING, FEELING, AND ACTING

Attention is the controlling factor in consciousness. The line followed by attention determines the course of thought and action. Several ideas may be in the margin of consciousness at the same time. They may be presented through the senses or revived by association. Only the one among these ideas to which attention is directed will get into the clear center of consciousness. The ideas which do not receive attention soon drop out of mind. The idea on which attention is directed remains longer in consciousness than it otherwise would. It becomes more clearly perceived, and becomes the dominant factor in determining the trend of association. Various ideas, associated with the one the attention is thus focused upon, may come more or less clearly

Attention Directs Mind's Activities

into consciousness, but the one of these which the attention selects will in turn become dominant in the train of thought.

In selecting the ideas which will come into mind, the attention controls the feelings which pervade consciousness, and the choices it makes, or the acts of will it performs. In more technical language, the attention, in exercising its selective function, controls the direction of thinking, feeling, and volitional acting.

The above applies to conscious processes in which association alone is depended upon to supply the ideas which come into mind. The conditions are modified somewhat when the salesman is presenting arguments and making suggestions to action. The arguments and suggestions displace ideas which would naturally come through association alone. But the arguments and suggestions have influence in controlling conscious processes and behaviour, only as they are selected by the attention.

ACTS OF WILL, OR IDEO-MOTOR ACTIVITY

One performs, as a matter of course, any act upon the doing of which he focuses his attention, unless he is prevented from doing it by some idea opposed to doing it, which is at the same time present in consciousness. Such a preventing idea is known in psychology as an inhibiting idea, and the prevention is known as inhibition.

The reader can readily find illustration of the motor tendency of ideas. Let him recall a recent trip to a store. Suppose he vividly imagines himself going to a store to make a purchase. If he tries to picture to himself in detail the actions involved, he feels himself actually beginning to perform the motions required to open the door, examine the article, etc. He will feel tendencies to activity in his vocal organs as he imagines himself speaking to the clerk.

The idea of performing an action tends to work itself out into action, that is, it is also an impulse to action. The ideas of purchasing which a salesman puts into a customer's mind are impulses to make the purchase.

Let us consider an example of an impulsive act which is fully performed. If one sees a child about to walk in front of a rapidly approaching car, he will reach out to pull him back. The act will be performed impulsively without stopping to think about

ACTS OF WILL 151

it. The thing seen arouses a strong feeling and suggests an act felt to be demanded by the situation. The impulse to perform the act fills consciousness so that all ideas of acting otherwise are excluded. In such a case the act is performed without other act of will, or volitional fiat.

The following illustrates how an inhibiting idea prevents an impulse from passing over into action. If one saw a child fall into deep water, he would feel a strong impulse to jump in to rescue him. If he could not swim, the situation would suggest to him the uselessness of carrying out the impulse. The idea of the uselessness of the act would doubtless prevent him from performing it. Such a preventing idea is technically known as an inhibiting idea. An objection which prevents a customer from closing is such an inhibiting idea.

ACTS OF WILL INVOLVING DELIBERATION

When two or more different lines of action are open to us, we may find it difficult to choose between them. Suppose it is a question whether I shall accept employment with another firm, or remain with the one for which I am now working. Each position has certain advantages and disadvantages. To bring these clearly into view, I endeavor to estimate fully the consequences which will follow upon each line of choice. Among them would be the prospects for permanent employment, increase of earnings, promotion, etc. The advantages of accepting the new position are compared with the advantages of the present employment. Finally, I come to the conclusion that one position offers, on the whole, more desirable prospects than the other. I turn my attention from the less attractive alternative and fix it on the more desirable one. In so doing the decision, or act of choice, is made. I accept the position which I have come to regard as the better.

Deliberation between alternatives is necessary for deliberate action. But carried too far, it paralyzes effort. The active, energetic, practically successful type of man is one who makes sure that all the essential facts bearing on the situation have been given due consideration. He then cuts loose from all but one line of action accepted as the most desirable. He concentrates all his energies on carrying out the chosen course.

THINKING

The line of development which mental processes follow is determined by a more or less explicit aim, or purpose, which the person desires and strives to realize. Thinking takes place when one becomes conscious of a not immediately realizable end he desires to attain. The thinking takes the form of casting about for ways and means of attaining the desired end.

When one encounters an obstacle to the attainment of a purpose, a state of stress or effort is aroused in his mind. The anticipated attainment of the desired end arouses a feeling of satisfaction and striving toward the end. The less satisfactory present state, contrasting with the desired one, arouses a feeling of aversion, or striving away from it. In a consciousness of obstructed attainment of purpose, a state of mingling desire and aversion is thus found. A feeling of hostility to the obstacle is also experienced. This stimulates the effort to get around the obstacle, or overcome it, or even to destroy it. One has reached a thought crisis which demands clear and effective thinking, rather than blind yielding to any one of the various impulsive feeling aspects of desire, as the state as a whole is generally called.

Any activity is said to be interesting, or to arouse a feeling of satisfaction, when it awakens within us the feeling that we are accomplishing something worth while; whether the "something" is very clearly defined or not. A feeling of interest is aroused by the consciousness of making progress toward the attainment of a desired end. The feeling of interest is a warming up to the activity, and at the same time a propensity to continue the activity which promises to satisfy the interest. The feelings of aversion and hostility lose in strength as the feeling that one is "getting warm" and the foretaste of the anticipated satisfaction grow stronger.

The desired end may be near or remote in the order of events. When the end is remote, it may be necessary, in order to attain it, to formulate many nearer ends which are subsidiary to it. The remote end then serves as a guide, or norm, in formulating the nearer ends, and in correlating and co-ordinating the efforts to attain them.

The efficient worker devotes his efforts continuously and persistently to the things and aims which he believes will play an important part in the attainment of his larger purposes. Efficiency requires that the non-essentials be eliminated. It demands that our aims or purposes be appraised according to the contribution to well-being that may be secured by attaining them. The efficient person cultivates a knowledge of, and desire for, the things worth while. He works to attain the things which give the richer and more enduring forms of satisfaction.*

*See discussion of "Well-Being or Self-Realization."

THINKING 155

Thinking always has a purpose or end in view. This purpose is to secure satisfaction for an instinct or interest. The origin and nature of the various interests, and the different lines of activity in which they seek satisfaction will be discussed later. The end which is held in view in thinking is felt to be desired. The end which it is desired to attain through the thinking processes is to bring about such an ordering of conscious experiences as will best satisfy the awakened interest or felt need.

Thinking occurs only when one becomes aware of an obstruction or hindrance to securing the satisfaction of the interest or need. There is the consciousness that one faces a problematic situation which must be solved before a desired end can be gained.

The problematic situation may consist essentially of the awareness that the end is not clearly enough comprehended and formulated and correlated with other ends to permit one to work definitely and efficiently toward its attainment. For example the problems of promoting welfare work among employees are largely of this character. Efforts along this line are often largely ineffective, because the one putting them forth does not clearly and adequately apprehend what definite ends must be attained in order that the welfare may be promoted satisfactorily. The ideal in doing welfare work should be to promote the harmonious satisfaction of the various interests of the employee involved in a fully developed personality. Success in the work will involve seeing to it that the employee has such incentive, wisdom, means, and opportunity as will enable him to secure such satisfaction.

If the purpose of the thinking is to overcome the difficulties in the way of accomplishing a definite mechanical result, or of performing some act such as selling an article, the problem may consist in selecting appropriate means and in employing them skillfully in the attainment of the clearly formulated purpose.

The first step in effective thinking and acting is to formulate and find answers to definite and pertinent questions. What is the end, or purpose, or aim, or goal, I wish to reach? What is the character of the obstacles that have obstructed the flow of my activities? Will this, that, or the other suggested answer be of assistance in solving the perplexity?

When one has clearly perceived his problem, the next step is to make a careful analytic search for the elements which have a significant bearing on the solution. The criterion for the selection and rejection of materials available, is their fitness for use as a means for attaining the desired end. The features of the materials which make them fit for this use are the qualities which give them significance for the end in view. The next step is the selection and arrangement of the significant features in such a way that they will contribute to the realizing of the end in view.

In the process of thinking, the interest or purpose dominant in consciousness at the time, through the

THINKING 157

form of activity known as attention or volition, exercises a selective control over the stream of thought. The interest exercises this selective control by determining on which of the various ideas coming into the margin of consciousness the spotlight of attention shall be focused. When this control is being effectively exercised, only such ideas are received into the clear center of attention as are believed to be relevant in some way to the end which the thinking is endeavoring to gain. It becomes interesting for this reason.

The interesting idea which is received into the focus of consciousness is more vividly perceived and remains longer in mind than the marginal ideas which are merely accorded a passing glance. The interesting aspect thus held in the clear center of consciousness becomes dominant in determining the ideas which will next come into mind through association.

As the ideas recalled through association appear above the threshold of consciousness they are noticed. If they appear to have no bearing on the business of the moment, they are given no further recognition. They remain withering in the dim margin for a brief moment, as they drop out of the mind.

If the idea occurring seems to have a bearing on the desired solution, the attention is fixed upon it. It is critically examined and fitted into its proper place in the thought system which is being constructed. If the solution is not readily reached, an attempt is made to hold all apparently relevant ideas in the background of consciousness. In this way there is built up a fringe, or constellation, of ideas mutually helpful in suggestive force, in the hope that one, or all of them, will finally suggest the solution the judgment approves.

When an interest or purpose thus controls the processes of thinking, it lapses into the background of consciousness. The attention is directed to the ideas that appear in the foreground, discriminating, measuring, and accepting or rejecting them. But the purpose must not be allowed to lapse entirely out of mind or thought will be deflected from its guidance.

The purpose of controlling the development of conscious processes, remains in the background, but its influence pervades and gives coherence to the flow of thoughts, feelings, and strivings. Figuratively speaking, it is the commanding officer viewing, and appraising, and ordering the whole field of conscious activities. Though it occupies a position on the field of action it is aloof from the various activities and vicissitudes of the actual contestants. The associative and logical thought processes are employed merely to serve the purposive processes of feeling and striving, just as the soldiers and the equipment of the army are used as a means of accomplishing the aim of the general.

In active thinking, as has been said, one has a

definite aim, or purpose, or problem in mind. He is searching for a means of gaining the end or solving the problem. Success in overcoming the difficulty encountered depends absolutely on the ideas which come to the mind through association. Success will depend upon the care and skill previously exercised in organizing knowledge into association systems.

Efficient thinking and doing must be founded on and spring from efficient learning. The process of learning efficiently was previously explained. Such learning consists in organizing the materials of knowledge into such forms of associative systems as will contribute most satisfactorily to the use of the materials in gaining satisfaction for the interests concerned with them. In such learning, the interest to be served by the organization must be kept alive in the margin of consciousness and must be firmly associated with the organized elements with which it is concerned, by concentrating attentive effort on firmly establishing the association.

The truly efficient man is the one who can see problems where others are unaware of them. He has cultivated a questioning and critical attitude of mind toward the affairs with which his activites are concerned. He is able to bring a well organized intelligence to the solution of the problems he thus discovers. Such a man has real initiative and brings about improvement and progress. Efficiency in business involves first, the adequate formulation of the ends to be striven for. One must then locate the obstacles in the way of attaining the ends. He must clearly perceive, and select, and skillfully employ the best means available for overcoming the difficulties and gaining the end.

In order to think and act adequately about a situation or proposition, he must have developed keen powers of discernment which enable him to select focus of attention. Right thinking and acting require that elements not relevant be disregarded, and that relevant matters be kept in mind until the means or way to the end is found. If one has previously fitted himself to handle the situation and keeps his attention concentrated on significant qualities or points, he will find coming into mind, through association, ideas which will guide him to a wise course of action.

One can have fertility and resourcefulness in thinking, only as he has previously established an extensive system of associations organized in accordance with their significant features. Fortunate is he who can see the significance of things, and can recall them when their significance will make them useful! The thinking of one whose knowledge is so organized will be significant rather than superficial. He will not be led off into inconsiderate action by the first plausible suggestion which occurs to him. He will be freely supplied with suggestions along alternative lines, which will lead him to carefully examine and appraise the superficially plausible suggestion.

When the suggestions do not come through the

associations previously established, one should undertake a systematic search for them. This search may take the form of carefully planned experiments or investigations of some sort. Or one may seek help in the experience of others through conversation or reading.

The solution of the problematic situation may thus demand that one acquire new learning. To avoid the uncertainty and tremendous loss involved in learning mainly by the method of blind trial and error, one should give an intelligent and searching investigation to the factors which may have significance for the solution of the problem. The number of failures in thinking and acting can thus be greatly reduced, but not entirely eliminated. The wider and more intelligently organized the past experience has been, the more effectively can be brought to bear on finding a way to overcome the difficulties of a novel situation.

TEST OF TRUTH

The more clearly one has centered his attention on methods of procedure, and has discriminated them from their context, and associated them with the general conditions under which they can be applied, the more effectively he will be able to bring the previously learned methods to bear in dealing with a novel situation.

Novel problems must be solved in terms of previous experiences, by combining or using the elements of such experience in new ways. One must search either his own experience or the experience of others for factors bearing on the solution of his problem. It is a difficult task to select the few significant factors in the problematic situation from the the significant aspects and hold them clearly in the many irrelevant features which are manifested along with them. When these are found it is still more difficult to form the right hypothesis, or theory, of dealing with them, than it is to determine whether we are on the right track to the solution, after the hypothesis has been formed. The only method of procedure is to critically examine the various possible solutions suggested. The most promising of these solutions should be selected as an hypothesis. By study and trial, or experimentation, one must endeavor to ascertain whether the tentatively accepted hypothesis offers the best way out of the difficulty. The test as to whether the true solution has been reached is whether it will guide us satisfactorily in dealing with the elements of experience so that we can attain our purpose. If we find that it works satisfactorily we accept it. If not, we reject it.

Whether a suggested solution, or tentative hypothesis, is correct can be determined only by testing it in subsequent experience. However, one can often arrive at a high degree of probability by carefully thinking out the consequences that can be foreseen as likely to follow such an attempt at verification in experience. In imagination, one can anticipate the results of experience. If the situation does not involve too novel elements, he can reach a reasonable certainty that his forecast of consequences is essentially correct. This is the process of verification; whether we are searching for general notions which will enable us to deal with presented materials, or whether we are searching for a particular means of attaining a general end. One by imaginatively testing his solutions in experience can form a conclusion that they are probably true. He should not make the mistake of regarding them as certainly true, until they have been actually tried out in experience.

JUDGMENT AND REASONING.

When one discriminates the various thought relations among the elements of experience he is said to pass judgment upon them. So also when a choice is made and a decision is reached after deliberating over the consequences of following different lines of action, the act is known as a judgment.

The function of judgment, as an element in the process of thinking, or reasoning, is to notice the significant relations existing among the objects of thought. Among the significant relations are **resemblances** and differences, the relation, of means to end, individual to class, cause and effect, the estimation of merit or value, and the discrimination of various other relations between ideas.

One passes judgment on a thing when he decides that it's value is equal to or greater than that of some other thing, or when he decides that he can use it to bring about an effect he desires to produce, or concludes that a certain effect has resulted from a cause of such and such a character, etc.

The salesman's task is largely to induce the man he solicits to pass judgment that the article offered is the best available means of securing some end which he desires to attain. He will then desire the thing as a means of attaining the desired end. In bringing this about the salesman has produced a

JUDGMENT AND REASONING 165

state of conviction or belief in the customer's mind.

Reasoning involves a series, or chain, of judgments. There are two forms of reasoning, known as induction and deduction. One is reasoning inductively when he derives general principles or conclusions from observed facts. If the salesman can show that this, that, and the other business man belonging to a certain class has found it profitable to use in his business the article offered for sale, he arrives inductively to the general principle, or conception, that the article will be found profitable by all men of that class.

The salesman can apply deductively the general principle thus established inductively. He does so if he convinces the men he is soliciting that the circumstances, conditions, and methods of his business will rightly bring him under the general class of profitable users. If the customer is convinced of this, he will conclude that what has proved profitable to others similarly situated will also be profitable to him. His belief is founded on his acceptance of the truthfulness and validity of the evidence on which the general principle of profitableness was established, and the conviction that the circumstances in which he finds himself, will rightly put him in the class of profitable users.

It may be well for a salesman to understand the method of procedure in deductive and inductive thinking, but he will hardly find it profitable to apply them in the formal way above illustrated. However, the salesman should understand that what is known as creating desire is generally merely showing that the object is an important member of a class of objects habitually regarded as desirable.

Our satisfied customers are our best advertisement, is a statement which aims by suggestion to cause the hearer, or reader, to make the inference and draw the same conclusion, which was reached above by following formal logical processes more closely. Such a suggestive statement is usually more effective than cold logic in influencing to action.

Such a suggestion may be backed up by a few reasons why. Even when such is the case, the one who is influenced by it is not moved by formal logical processes to make a fully reasoned choice. He is rather moved by suggestion to perform an act of rational imitation. This subject is developed more fully in discussing suggestion and imitation in the "Psychology for Business Efficiency" and the "Psychology of Advertising."

It must be remembered that thoughts originate, or grow, only from one's own experience, past and present. One is skillful in judging, as his past experience has been rich and varied, and skillfully organized and assimilated. One, so prepared, can readily select the right idea and apply it accurately in solving the problems at hand.

The genius is one who clearly perceives the significant aspects and relations of things and links them together, and to the related parts of his experience,

JUDGMENT AND REASONING 167

by helpful associations. The expert has reflected on experience, has studied and classified actual and hypothetical cases, and has formed useful association systems. He thus has many fully formed conclusions and principles of action stored away in his memory. As soon as the essential facts of a new proposition are clearly established, he at once recognizes it as belonging to a class with which he is already familiar. Without apparent consideration, or deliberation, the expert, thus prepared, can immediately and confidently give a decision on matters of the utmost importance. He has previously gone through the processes of investigation and deliberation. He sees his way clearly at once, and is ready to act confidently in accordance with his judgment. A selling appeal addressed to an expert should take a different form from one addressed to an inexperienced buyer.

BELIEF AND ACTION

Deliberation results normally in conviction, belief, and action. If I am convinced, or believe, that it will rain, I shall carry an umbrella; unless, taking everything into consideration, I am convinced, or believe that getting wet will involve less inconvenience than carrying the umbrella. In either case the belief determines the action.

I am always ready to act along the line which I believe will contribute most to the realization of the purpose which at the time seems to me most important. Because it seems most important, my attention is fixed upon it, or rather it holds my attention.

Deliberation and reasoning aim to eliminate rivalry and conflict among impulses to action. Deliberation is brought to a close when order and harmony are established among the impulses to action. When a decision has thus been reached, one refuses to attend to suggestions arousing impulses to act along an opposing line.

In attending to the acts appropriate to the conviction or belief established, he sets the switches for their performance. At last, when all preparations are made, and the judgment declares that the time and circumstances are ripe for the believed in action, and that the line is open, then the act is performed as a matter of course.

PART III

FACTORS WHICH DETERMINE THINKING, FEELING, AND ACTING

INSTINCTS OR PREDISPOSITIONS

Some parts of the following discussion of interests may seem very difficult to one who has not studied psychology. The relative importance of the subject is fully as great as its difficulty. This fact should stimulate the reader to put forth the effort necessary to grasp it. It goes to the core of the motives which influence action. The mastery of this part of the subject should helpfully illuminate the work of the salesman. It is of fundamental significance in the widely prevalent effort to rightly motivate education, vocation, and other activities of life.

"The Classification of Interests", and most that follows it, will be easier. The application of psychological principles in the practice of salesmanship will become clearer if one has a thorough understanding of the interests and the part they play in determining the actions of men. The significance of the harder parts of the book will be better understood on a second reading. If the psychology of salesmanship were easy, many books would have been written on the subject long before this.

Men are moved to action by impulses which have their roots in instincts. These instincts originated in very remote evolutionary processes because of their usefulness in promoting the welfare of the individual, or of the community to which he belonged, and in perpetuating the race. The social reformer, the politician, the teacher, the preacher, the advocate, or the salesman can influence men only by appealing to emotions, sentiments or interests developed from these instincts.

The salesman who attempts to awaken interest and desire will be greatly assisted by understanding the origin, nature and significance of these mental processes and the part they play in influencing the actions of men. One who has this knowledge will be better able to arouse interest and desire for his proposition and to take advantage of their impelling force.

An eminent authority has defined an instinct as an inherited, or innate, mental and physical predisposition to experience an impulse to attend to certain things, to feel desire or aversion for them, and to act in a predetermined way in regard to them. An instinct is complicated, purposive behaviour which has not been acquired or learned through educational processes.

From the physiological point of view a predisposition is a complex constellation of nervous paths. These paths may be fully pre-formed or partially pre-formed. That is, they may exist in a fully de-

INSTINCTS 171

veloped form previous to experience, or they may be only partially pre-developed and hence require experience to perfect them.

On the psychological side a predisposition is a capacity and tendency to feel interest in and strive for. Physical predispositions may be fully pre-developed or partially pre-developed.

On the psychical side the predispositions have various qualities, attributes, or characteristics which distinguish the various processes of being interested. In their developed form they take on the differentiations which are distinguished in and predicated of the conscious processes. The qualities or characteristics observed in objects awaken certain correlated mental processes of feeling, interest, and striving which have distinguishable qualities or characteristics.

When one becomes aware of the object which is the stimulus to which a certain form of instinctive behaviour is the appropriate response, he feels a strong impulse and desire to perform the instinctive act. When one first performs the instinctive act he is probably not aware of the purpose which his behaviour serves to attain. Even if he has a certain sort of vague, innate fore-knowledge of the general end to be gained, it is evident that the awareness of the purpose does not determine the form of the behaviour. There is no deliberate effort to determine what to do, or why to do it, or what is the best form of behaviour under the circumstances. When such factors enter into the performance, the act is not a perfectly developed instinct. It results rather from more or less definite instinctive tendencies and capabilities.

The instinctive endowment of man consists largely of general tendencies and capabilities. Even such perfectly developed instincts as he has, cease to be blind as one grows in experience. With the growth of experience, the real purpose of the instinctive act comes into view and determines the choice of means to attain it. The original instinctive behaviour, or reaction to stimulus, is greatly modified. Such modification is often necessary to adapt the act properly to the circumstances in which the individual finds himself. This is true largely because the conditions of human life have changed greatly from those of the remote evolutionary period in which the instinct originated.

Authorities vary greatly in the number of instincts they enumerate. As was said before, some of the innate tendencies and capabilities of human beings are not manifested in the form of perfectly developed instincts. They require development through education and experience. However, most authorities will agree in the broad view that man, as the result of the inherited structure and tendencies to development in his psychical and physical organism, is predisposed to do a much larger number of things than are the lower animals.

ENUMERATION OF INSTINCTS

Taking the broad view, the following are among the more important instinctive capabilities or tendencies:

Appetite for certain foods and disgust for others, anger, hate, affection, rivalry, emulation, jealousy, shyness, fear, teasing, self-assertion, modesty, sexual love, parenthood, desire for approbation, sympathy, imitation, play and recreation, fighting, nomadism, agriculture (making things grow), hunting, constructiveness, secretiveness, inquisitiveness (curiosity (or desire to know), acquisitiveness, the predatory instinct, artistic interest, respect for others, gregariousness, co-operation with others, loyalty to group interest, subordination to superiors, morality, and religion, or self-subjection to the Divine Will.

The following are brief illustrations of the sort of behaviour to which some of these instincts lead. The setting hen feels that she simply must set, even if the nest is empty. Whether a brood of chickens will result from her setting evidently does not influence her act. The instincts in a human being can not long remain as "blind" as this. However, the boy may unquestionably follow an impulse to collect articles of no real value. So one sex is attracted to the other, and so the man may feel an overwhelming impulse to go fishing, or hunting.

The innate predispositions play an important part in ordering the affairs of life. One instinctively fears whatever threatens to prevent the attainment of a desire.

The consciousness of being alone in the dark or in a vast wilderness may arouse an instinctive fear, which is none the less genuine, though one recognizes that there is nothing to harm him. We hate a person who maliciously hinders the attainment of our purpose. Emulation impels an individual to rival the achievements of a superior. Rivalry, developed to excess, grows into envy, jealousy, anger, and hate. We are jealous of persons whom we regard as our rivals. We envy them their success. Acquisitiveness leads to competition and rivalry. It leads to envy, when the thing desired belongs to another. One is envious of a person when he covets his goods, and may become jealous of him as a successful rival for the goods.

Secretiveness impels one to conceal his business from others. Its instinctive character is shown by the fact that it often influences one when there is no real reason for concealment. Curiosity, or inquisitiveness, is interest in knowing. In business, curiosity, or interest in knowing about a thing, should be clearly distinguished from acquisitiveness, or interest in securing it. Curiosity may be made to lead to acquisitiveness, if proper advantage is taken of it. Combativeness may be dangerously strengthened by an extreme militaristic policy, or dangerously weakened by a peace at any price attitude.

Sympathy is the general instinctive tendency to experience an emotion perceived to be manifested in others. One responds as instinctively to the observed expression of an emotion, as he does to the object which is fitted to arouse the emotion, and for similar reasons. The instinctive imitation of the expression of the emotional state makes one aware of the nature of the state, by arousing a corresponding emotion in him. This emotion aroused through imitation is accompanied by an impulse to carry it out into appropriate behaviour. The person who experiences and responds to an emotion through instinctive imitation may be totally unaware of the stimulus which aroused the instinctive response in the person imitated. This has been a source of advantage as when the instinctive response has, for example, enabled one to escape a danger of which he was unaware. It may also lead to destructive panics and other detrimental acts. Through this instinct the enthusiasm and confidence of the salesman arouse similar feelings in his customer.

One instinctively reacts to the expression of an emotion which he has inspired in another. The suggestive force of one's own expression is reflected back to him and adds strength to his already strong feeling. As each one of a crowd is thus influencing and in turn being influenced by others, the emotions may be worked up to a very intense form. The sympathetic, reciprocating, cumulative spread of an emotion through imitation accounts for the fact that the emotion a person experiences when witnessing a play as one of a large crowd is much greater than he would experience as the only spectator. The expression of pleasure or displeasure by the various members of an audience tend mutually to heighten each other. More will be said on this subject later.

Instincts do not appear until the necessary nervous connections have developed through bodily growth. No two children manifest exactly similar instincts. They vary in number, in relative strength, and in time and order of manifestation. All the instincts will appear sooner or later in a normal person, if a suitable stimulus is experienced when the nervous system has reached a proper stage of development.

In a general way, the human instincts have tended to adjust the individual to the necessary conditions of his existence. They enable him, independently of education, to make his environment contribute in some measure to the satisfaction of his needs.

In man the instinctive preadjustment has never attained to the perfection which it has reached in the lower animals. In the animals the instincts are ready made capabilities to perform certain acts. They are, compartively speaking, modified or improved but little by education. In man the instincts are largely tendencies and capacities which must be developed into capabilities and habits through education.

INSTINCTS REQUIRE EDUCATIONAL DIRECTION

It is not safe for the individual to follow blindly the guidance of his native impulses. Pugnacity may be taken as an illustration. The fighting spirit, as developed in some militaristic circles, is harmful to the interests of society as a whole. Yet there is no doubt that a refined and tempered form of the fighting spirit is essential to the attainment of great achievements.

An instinct may develop into a good or bad habit, or die out from lack of exercise. It may be so strong as to lead readily to over development. Or it may be weak and require strong stimulation and much exercise.

As a result of stimulation and exercise the instincts are correlated and developed into habits. In their developed forms they manifest themselves as interests and temperamental traits of character.

An instinctive tendency may fail to develop into an element of character, because of the lack of an appropriate stimulus, or of an opportunity to perform the act: or the failure to develop may result from the fact that one yields so fully to some one instinct that he neglects to exercise others. Or the instinct may be forcibly repressed. While a merely neglected instinct may die out, one that is forcibly repressed may merely become dormant and manifest itself in some foolish or perverted act later in life.

It is the business of the educational agencies, among which the parents occupy a very important position, to see that proper stimuli and opportunities for exercise are furnished to each instinct when it ripens. In this way the instinct may be developed into an interest or trait of character useful to the individual.

The instincts are often in rivalry with each other. The educator must see that they are properly harmonized. He must also see that the person is furnished with knowledge and incentive to guide his development along the lines of his real needs.

The mental constitution of an individual has taken its form through the development in the evolutionary experienec of ancestors. This constitution includes the rather specific instincts we have mentioned. It also includes more general innate capacities and powers which are more variable in their manifestations in individuals than the more specific instincts.

Among such qualities we may mention, as examples, the capacity for more than ordinary achievement in science, business, mathematics, politics, painting, music, etc. The possession of such capacities apparently does not result entirely from the inheritance of a practically perfect nervous organization. They appear to be, in large part, innate

EDUCATION OF INSTINCTS

mental tendencies, qualities, and capacities. The inborn capacities must be developed into capabilities through education. The born salesman needs education to fully develop his ability. This inherited mental constitution determines largely the trend of the development of the nervous organization acquired during the life of the individual. An instinct acquired during remote evolutionary experience is a trace of that experience persisting in the mental and physical constitution of the individual. This innate trace of remote racial experience is comparable to a memory of such experience. Through these traces the lessons of past experience indelibly impressed on the mental and physical constitution of the individual are operative in guiding him through present experience.

In the instinctive striving there may be, previous to actual experience, some faint perception of the end at which the impulse aims. In the fear instinct this preperception may take the form of a very imperfectly defined "Danger—there! This way to escape!" In carrying out an instinct, the stimulating object is regarded as a thing with which one is greatly concerned. There is certainly present also the feeling that something worth while is being gained by the behaviour.

The awareness of why the act is worth while could arise only through the awakening of innate knowledge along with the innate feeling and impulse.

The traces of previous experience preserved in

the mental constitution and manifested as instincts work through more or less perfectly preformed pathways of neural discharge. The less perfectly or less completely these pathways are organized, the more important is the function performed by the traces of past experience existing in consciousness, and the more necessary it is to develop intelligence to guide in the response to the stimulus.

MODIFICATION OF INSTINCTS

Instinctive behaviour may be analyzed into the following important elements: The perception of an object which serves as the stimulus; the emotion and impulse aroused by the stimulus; the form of behaviour which results as the response to the stimulus.

One may learn to improve the instinctive response to a stimulus. He may learn to discriminate the circumstances under which he should make the response, from those under which he should not make it. He may, through experience, associate with the object which first called forth the response, another feeling and impulse which will lead to a different response. "The burnt child dreads the fire." One may learn to respond instinctively to objects which at first failed to arouse such a response.

An instinct may be modified by associating with the object and the feeling it arouses another form of response. The response to the feeling and the impulse aroused by the stimulus is shunted off into another line of action. In this way one may be led

MODIFICATION OF INSTINCTS

to make the conventional rather than the primitive response to the stimulus. Actions are thus made to conform to the forms of conduct prescribed by society. The sex instincts, for example, require such modification.

Instincts may be modified by refining, sublimating, generalizing, and co-ordinating them. The gregarious, co-operating, and fighting instincts and those of emulation, play, etc., are thus modified by properly conducted sports. One who fights for victory according to the rules of the game is likely to become one who fights the battles of business and political life in accordance with the principles which should govern conduct in those spheres.

WILL TO LIVE

In the earliest form of conscious life there was probably simply a vague consciousness of impulsive-process-going-on and of satisfaction-accompany-the-going-on. It was the will to live seeking and finding satisfaction in the conscious-impulsive-satisfying-activity which constituted the process of living.

The general will to gain satisfaction through carrying out impulse has come, through the process of evolution, to manifest itself along many different lines. The various instinctive predispositions serve to guide impulsive activities into the lines along which they most profitably seek for satisfaction. They are differentiations of the original capability of experiencing impulse and of feeling satisfaction in carrying it out. As such they must be dominated and correlated by the general will so that they will work together harmoniously, each contributing duly to the satisfaction of all.

INSTINCT OF SELF-REALIZATION

We have found that we can trace one all inclusive, all pervasive instinct manifesting itself in the various special instincts. We may call this the instinct of self-realization. It is essentially a process of seeking satisfaction through carrying out impulse.

In one aspect, the instincts are processes of reacting to the environment. The form of the reaction is determined by a correlation existing between certain objects of consciousness and certain qualities in the physical and mental constitution of the individual. In another aspect, since the behaviour resulting from the stimulus is determined by the psychical and physical constitution, this behaviour may be regarded as a form of self expression.

The instincts are predispositions to act in such ways as will best promote one's well-being, or self-realization. The instinct of self-realization works blindly at first, groping its way by mere impulse. As man's experience widens and as his intelligence increases, the character of this predominating instinct becomes more clearly revealed. It develops into an ideal of well-being. The ideal is that of a form of well-being to be attained by developing all one's capacities into capabilities of securing satisfaction and of exercising these capabilities, each with due regard to the other, and of safeguarding them.

Some of the instincts aim largely at making one's material environment subservient to the progressive approximation to the ideal of well-being or self-realization. Among them are constructiveness and acquisitiveness.

Other instincts, such as play, curiosity, and especially imitation, have for their purpose the improvement of well-being through giving a better mastery of the objects of both the material and social environments so that they may be employed more efficiently as means of securing satisfaction.

Some of the instincts concerned with the social environment are egoistic or seek for the well-being of one's self. Some are altruistic and seek for the well-being of others. Some are antisocial, others are pro-soical.

Among the egoistic or self seeking instincts are pugnacity, fear, self assertion, rivalry, shyness, secretiveness.

Teasing and the predatory instinct are antisocial.

The altruistic instincts are general pro-social. That is, they aim at promoting the well-being of others. Such are parenthood, sympathy, modesty, sexual love, respect for others, co-operation, gregariousness, loyalty, and subordination to superiors.

No man can come into being or develop his capacities apart from others. Born into collective life man's well-being must be brought about through co-operation with others, in collective life. The will to live in its various lines of instinctive development clearly aims at self-realization in the give and receive of association with others. The state of well-being aimed at is a state of social well-being in which each will profit in proportion to his service to others, and only as he renders such service. The supreme good is a common good, to be attained in a community, the members of which are mutually dependent and mutually helpful. One just as naturally feels regard for the collective welfare, as for his individual welfare.

The striving for self-realization is a striving for

such a condition of collective well-being as we have just explained. The ideal of self-realization has been formulated through co-operative experience and co-operative reflection on experience. It is an end not fully attainable, but to which we can always approach more closely.

Man is a social being with broadly diversified interests and concerns, as well as a marvelous machine for performing work. His well-being can be promoted only by providing opportunities and stimuli leading to the satisfaction of his various lines of interest. This fact should be kept in mind in planning welfare work.

MORAL INTEREST

The instinct of self-realization has developed into the interest of self-realization, which is known as the moral interest. This moral interest is an interest in well-being, or in well-doing, as being is in this sense a process of doing. In a condition of well-being, or well-doing, all of one's interests, both egoistic and altruistic, would be developed in proportion to his true needs. All of these interests would be satisfied with due regard to the well-being of the organic individual whole, of which they are characteristics. It is a condition in which one gains a harmonious satisfaction for interests which have been developed in proportion to needs.

Moral acts are acts which concern the social well-being. Acts which affect the efficiency of any individual member of society, affect the well-being of the society of which he is a member. Society must see that its various members keep themselves in a condition to render efficient service, just as a person must see to it that his various organs are working properly. Hence society lays down rules to which the behaviour of the individual must conform.

The moral judgment is the judgment of society, which has followed and handed down, in tradition and custom the best judgments of the moral leaders of the past. This judgment voices the collective racial experience as to acts which tend to hinder or promote the individual and social well-being.

By our instinctive endowment we are sensitive to the praise and blame, or approval and disapproval of our fellows and conform largely to their will. Those who do not so conform are penalized in various ways. Through suggestion and imitation we accept the maxims and traditions in which are formulated the racial experience as to what is good or bad.

One gets his ideal of conduct as a suggestion from others. When he comes to see that this ideal aims at the true co-ordination of collective and individual welfare, he may strive to promote this welfare, regardless of the collective approval, or disapproval, of his acts.

The sentiments and impulses, which give force to the moral ideal in controlling conduct, have developed under educational influences from various altruistic and egoistic, instinctive tendencies. The moral ideal may thus be conceived as developing from impulses and capacities which have their origin in the Eternal Consciousness or Divine Spirit which is manifested in us.

The Universal Will to Live manifests itself in all living things. Its impulsive force becomes manifested along the lines of the various instinctive tendencies. In our conscious experiences we become aware of these native impulses and capacities. As experience develops, intelligence furnishes guidance in efforts to seek satisfaction for them. But the form into which the moral personality develops is determined mainly by social agencies.

The instinctive predispositions have been developed in the course of evolution as a means of promoting well-being. They are tendencies to feel and act in a certain way in regard to things which concern well-being. When one becomes aware of this concern with a thing, he experiences a desire and an impulse to strive for it, or an aversion and an impulse to strive away from it, according to whether it concerns his well-being favorably or unfavorably. The person is said to have an interest in the things which thus concern well-being.

The things which concern well-being similarly are arranged in a general class. General lines of concern come to be recognized. Around each line of concern, of which one becomes conscious, is organized a system of tendencies to feel and act. The habits of responding to such classes of objects with co-ordinated tendencies to feel and **act, are** known as interests. When an interest has been formed, as soon as an object is recognized as belonging to the general class, it arouses the desire and impulse characteristic of interest.

The individual is said to be adapted to his environment by his instinctive tendencies. However, these tendencies seem rather to be the agencies by which the environment is made to promote the satisfaction of the individual. The instincts act as guides before experience has been sufficiently developed to deal with things which concern well-being by furthering or hindering it. They guide one to the satisfaction of certain needs not yet felt to be such. Where the instincts are lacking in perfection or definiteness, consciousness steps in and undertakes to do what preformed structure has left undone, in the way of making the environment subservient to human interests.

Man grows gradually into a consciousness, or realization, that certain classes of things concern his well-being in certain ways. The ends toward which the instincts impel one come to be formulated as aims or purposes to be desired. The line which the development of the individual actually follows is a resultant, or mean, of two component factors. The two factors determining development are instinctive endowment and educational influence.

When the conscious realization of concern is awakened, it takes the form known as interest. Conscious processes are interesting when some capacity of the self is finding satisfaction in the activities. Man is impelled to action through a conception of himself as satisfied as the result of action. The foretaste of satisfaction, which arises from representing or picturing one's self as having gained the object, or attained the interesting or desired end, arouses the impulse to the action and leads to such a rearrangement of conditions as will bring about the anticipated satisfaction.

TWO MEANINGS OF INTEREST

The word interest is used in two different senses which should be distinguished from each other. In the wider meaning of the term, one is interested in all that concerns his need or welfare, though he may not be conscious of the concern. In this sense one may ignorantly do a thing contrary to his interest, if he is unaware of the effect the act will have on his well-being.

In the psychological sense, an interest is a conscious realization that a general class of things concerns one's need or well-being. The feeling of interest varies with the importance attributed to the thing as a means of affecting the well-being favorably or unfavorably.

The consciousness of favorable concern arouses a feeling of pleasure, a foretaste of the satisfaction to be attained, and a striving or impulse to attain it. This complex state is known as a desire.

The consciousness of unfavorable concern arouses

a feeling of pain, a foretaste of dissatisfaction, and an impulse of aversion, or a striving away from.

CLASSIFICATION OF INTERESTS

The experience of the race in working out the due co-ordination and satisfaction of the various interests has found that they may be dealt with most conveniently, in theory and in practice, when they are grouped in a few important classes.

In the fully developed consciousness, an interest as a motive impelling to action, will be found to have two aspects. In one aspect it is an interest in a special line of activity. In another aspect the special line of interest is a manifestation of the general interest in self realization which includes all other interests.

The all pervading and all inclusive interest in self realization or well-being, manifests itself in the moral interest. The moral interest is the interest in correlating and co-ordinating the special lines of interest. The special lines of interest include politico-legal, philanthropy, sociability, health, knowledge and educational skill, wealth, beauty, vocation, family and home and recreation.

The interests are the ends which the instincts serve, brought into clear consciousness, and developed into habitual lines of desiring and striving.

MORALITY—THE MAJOR INTEREST

The interest in general well-being, or in properly

co-ordinated satisfaction along the various lines of interest, is known as the moral interest. The feelings of interest which attach themselves to matters which concern general well-being, or self-realization, are known as feelings of oughtness, or obligation.

The feelings of rightness and wrongness attach themselves to acts which tend to further or hinder general well-being. These feelings are manifested at first as blind instinctive impulses. They predispose one to do the right act and not to do the wrong one.

Through educational development, which is guided by social influences, the feelings of obligation, or oughtness, tend to lose their blind instinctive character. As experience develops, one gains the ability to appraise the tendency of the acts to hinder or further general well-being. Wrong acts are seen to be acts which have bad results. Right acts are those which bring good results. However, the obligation feelings to which judgments of rightness and wrongness give rise, still retain their instinctively imperative character.

Goodness means fitness to promote well-being. A thing is good only as it is good for something. It is good only when it is adapted to serve as a means of attaining a good purpose. Goodness can be estimated only in relation to the end to be served. Good and bad things are things which have a favorable or unfavorable bearing on well-being.

CLASSIFICATION OF INTERESTS 193

The enlightened conscience aims at a progressively realized state of well-being, to be brought about through a happy adjustment, or co-ordination, and satisfaction of the egoistic interests, which have regard for self, and of the altruistic interests, which have regard for others. It aims to harmonize the various interests of the individual and the interests of society so as to achieve a higher and richer life for all. Conscience aims to bring the interests of the individual into harmony with the great social will, and with the Universal Will of which it is a manifestation.

Moral principles arise from the recognition that acts concern both individual and social well-being. They are general principles to which acts must conform in order to promote this well-being. They are rules for playing the game of life. The moral virtues are habits of acting in accordance with moral principles.

The principles to which acts should conform, in order that they may be regarded as moral, include, among others, honesty, truthfulness, fidelity, loyalty, justice, mercy, courage, industry, thrift, frugality, temperance, chastity, modesty. They are the principles by which impulses to action along the line of the various interests should be appraised, to see whether they should be held in check or strengthened.

PHILANTHROPY INTEREST

From the various predispositions to perform actions which promote the well-being of others has developed the interest in philanthropy. This interest has its roots in gregariousness, the parental instinct, the tender emotion, affection, sympathy, co-operation, loyalty to group interests, filial devotion, respect for others, self-subjection, religion, etc. It is the interest in rendering social service for which no service, or means of securing service, is to be received in exchange. This distinguishes it from business, which is the rendering of service for a consideration.

Many confuse philanthropy with the moral interest. However, philanthropy is merely one among several lines of well-doing with which the moral interest is concerned. The philanthropy interest must be co-ordinated and correlated with the sociability, health, education, wealth, beauty, recreation, vocation, family and home, and politico-legal interests, in accordance with moral principles. One is under obligation to develop and exercise his own capabilities along all these lines. He is also under obligation to provide, through exercise of his philanthropy interest, that others have opportunity and incentive to develop their interests along the same lines. The moral interest is coextensive with life interests.

CLASSIFICATION OF INTERESTS 195

POLITICO-LEGAL INTEREST

The politico-legal interest aims to render service to the individual and to society through organized co-operative effort. The political organization is the machinery employed for rendering this service. Through legislation the legal interest aims to enact the laws which will establish the form of organization which will be most efficient in promoting individual and collective well-being through co-operative effort.

The legal interest also aims to make laws which record the consensus of moral judgment, to establish judicial machinery to apply this judgment to concrete cases, and to provide for executives to enforce the judicial decisions.

FAMILY AND HOME INTEREST

The family interest aims at promoting the various interests of those for whom conjugal, or parental, or filial affection exists. The members of the family are interested in the home as a means of satisfying a great variety of interests.

Service to the home and family is the vocation of a large majority of women. It also makes large demands on women who have other vocations, and on all normal men.

The home interest embraces all the activities which aim at the well-being of the members of the home and all the things with which these activities are concerned. The home and family interest is concerned with things pertaining to domestic economy and domestic art. Among them are wholesome and appetizing food, architecture, heating, ventilating, and lighting, domestic art, decorations, furnishing, sewing and various forms of household activities which it is hardly necessary to mention. The home interest embraces all the home activities which aim at the well-being of the members of the home, and all the things with which the attainment of this well-being is concerned.

SOCIABILITY INTEREST

This interest impels one to strive to secure personal recognition along social, civic, political, business, and other lines. It gives rise to the ambition to be esteemed and reckoned with by one's fellows. Whatever gives one advantage in competition with others, or in influencing and leading others, or makes him looked up to, admired, or considered by others, appeals to this interest and will be desired when the social advantage to be gained by means of it is made clear.

For example, a new fashion is taken up as a means of securing social recognition, or prestige. What makes one appear well dressed is desired as a means of securing recognition from his business associates. See the discussion of "Fashion" in the "Psychology for Business Efficiency". Posting the names and records of the men who do the most ef-

CLASSIFICATION OF INTERESTS 197

fective work in a factory may stimulate others to do much better work in order to secure such recognition. This appeals to the instincts of emulation, rivalry, and self-assertion, which are elements of this interest.

HEALTH INTEREST

The health interest attaches itself to anything which prevents or cures disease, or prevents accident. It is concerned with wholesome food, water, light, ventilation, dwelling place, conditions of labor, physical culture, and athletics.

EDUCATION INTEREST

The educational interest is concerned with whatever increases knowledge, or wisdom, or makes for efficiency in economic, social, or political activities, or enlightens one as to a better means of self-realization along the line of any recognized interest. It makes for culture as its ideal. Culture is knowledge, appreciation, and utilization of the things which give enduring satisfaction.

ÆSTHETIC INTEREST

This is generally known as the interest in beauty. It is concerned with such things as the theater, literature, music, painting, sculpture, architecture, landscape gardening, beautifying the person, the home, and its furnishings, and surroundings, and with the beauty of natural objects, etc.

WEALTH INTEREST

The wealth interest aims at mastery of the material environment. Whatever increases ability to earn money, or save money, or reduces expenses, appeals to this interest.

It is a superficial and false ideal which makes the pursuit of wealth the supreme end in life. The attainment of wealth is not a true criterion of success. The amount of wealth attained is only one among several elements which must be taken into consideration in estimating business success. Riches acquired without adequate beneficial service rendered to others, in return for the wealth secured, is exploitation. It departs from the principle of the square deal, and is bad business.

The attainment of business success is only one element involved in attaining broad human success. The attainment of wealth is desirable mainly as a means of securing satisfaction along other lines of self-realization.

Two motives contribute largely to the effective performance of the economic activities of business. One motive is to meet the demands for service to the well-being of others, which the business aims to satisfy. This is the vocational interest. The other motive is to provide the means of satisfying not only the economic interests of the worker, but also his æsthetic, educational, sociability, health and recreation interests as well. The economic, or wealth,

CLASSIFICATION OF INTERESTS 199

interest is only one of several belonging to the same general class. These interests are manifested in many sub-varieties and combinations. The moral interest aims to so co-ordinate their various activities that all will receive a degree of satisfaction such as will make them contribute duly and harmoniously to collective well-being.

VOCATION INTEREST

In one aspect, the vocation interest is an interest in rendering to others service which will promote their well-being. The vocation interest aims also to make the rendering of service to others, a means of securing the things which will promote one's own well-being. The two motives working together aim at a mutually advantageous exchange of services, or of means of securing service.

Every one may rightly demand the satisfaction of his own interest in well-being, provided he renders an equivalent service in promoting the well-being of others.

Most people are under the necessity of making a living, in order that they may be able to meet their obligations to enrich the well-being of themselves and others. Vocational activities are directed along certain specific lines largely as a result of the fact that efforts to satisfy the needs must be correlated and concentrated along rather narrow lines, in order that they may become efficient and deserve and receive reward.

Work which is taken up merely because it affords an opportunity to make a living may lack qualities which are very essential to the satisfaction of the vocational interest. In order to gain due satisfaction for the vocational interest, one should specialize his efforts along some line in which he feels he is rendering value received to others in return for the compensation he receives for his work. Vocation should be chosen along lines of fitness to serve, not merely along the lines in which it is possible that the greatest financial returns may be secured for serving. The feeling that the activities are worth while helps make them interesting. The satisfaction which comes from doing worth-while things is one of the greatest rewards that service can gain.

Vocation means a calling to render service to others along the line for which one's abilities best fit him. The choice of a vocation is the selection and devotion of one's self to activities one feels called upon to perform. To be truly vocational, the activities should be interesting. The achievement of their end should bring satisfaction. An occupation which meets the demands of one's nature, and in which one's aptitudes and abilities fit him to be successful in rendering service to others, is the greatest source of lasting happiness.

Work which really meets the demands of the vocational interest may at first be neutral in feeling or even distasteful. Yet if the occupation, as a whole, is really felt to be worth while, much of the work will take on an acquired interest. It is more than likely that work, which as a whole satisfies the requirements of the vocational interest, will always be found to involve distasteful, or painful activities.

When one has chosen his vocation, he should say to himself: "This is my job. It is up to me to do it, or to be done for. I will do it."

Practical necessity usually compels one to confine his vocational activities to a rather narrow line. His vocation can not afford satisfaction along all the lines of his interests. It must be regarded as the means of securing that which can be used to secure satisfaction along avocational lines.

One's vocational activities do not completely fulfill his obligations to render service to others. Part of one's serious efforts at self-realization must be devoted to rendering service to others, for which the only compensation is the satisfaction resulting from the consciousness of the service rendered. One must render a vocational service to others, as individuals, and as members of family, political, civic, and other social groups.

To successfully perform serious work of the more important sort, intense voluntary concentration must be maintained for a considerable period of time. Such work involves dealing with theoretical or practical problems which must be solved in order to promote well-being. The problem may be concerned with adapting or employing external means to satisfy a felt need. Or, the problem may be of the intellectual sort which aims at satisfying the felt need for orderliness and consistency in our knowledge.

Being thwarted in the solution of a problem gives displeasure and adds to the fatigue of the work. A satisfactory solution of a problem, or the consciousness of progress toward a solution, gives pleasure. Such pleasure plays a wholesome part in the economy of life.

Even when work is rich in the amount of such pleasure it gives, it finally becomes fatiguing and demands periods for recuperation and recreation. The fatigue and the need for means of recuperation are much greater in lines of work which are largely routine and disagreeable in character.

WORK AND THE NEED FOR RECREATION

Work that is full of interest and pleasure finally becomes fatiguing and demands periods for recreation. Life grows wearisome as it follows the daily grind of routine in shop, or store, or home, even if the occupation, on the whole, is congenial. Such work may grow repulsive, if persisted in too long without interruption.

The dull rounds of some forms of monotonous toil become deadening in their humdrum influence. One may become so desperate as to be ready to resort even to crime to break the monotony, if no other means is available. Even if sufficient leisure is provided for rest and sleep, they alone are not sufficient to restore the exhausted energies of one employed in the more deadening occupations. Such a person can not come back to work with a wholesome feeling, unless some form of recreation is provided.

One employed regularly at a congenial occupation will have many interests not sufficiently exercised in his ordinary work. He will become conscious of the need of satisfying these interests.

The brain cells corresponding to various developed interests should be stimulated, to use up the accumulated energy. In this way alone can the capacity for supplying energy be kept in efficient working. Atrophy, or wasting away of capacity, follows disuse.

A disagreeable emotional tone arises from developed interests which are denied wholesome stimulation and satisfaction. A similar feeling results from interests so stimulated that an undue amount of energy is used up. Such an unpleasant emotion spreads a disagreeable feeling over vocational or avocational activities, which would otherwise have an agreeable tone. When work is monotonous or disagreable, the unpleasant feeling, arising from the understimulated or overstimulated interests, may add to the dislike for it to such an extent as to make it practically unbearable.

RECREATION INTEREST

The recreation interest plays a very important part in the activities of a well ordered life. This interest demands that vocational and avocational work must not be allowed to fill all one's time. One must have time to engage in the satisfaction of other interests. One must also have opportunity, and proper stimulus and incentive, to insure the exercise of otherwise neglected interests.

Recreation may be satisfactory in character, though it does not fully exercise all one's interests outside his regular line of work. Practical considerations generally make it necessary for one to seek his recreation along rather narrow lines of interest. The instinctive impulses leading to recreational activities thus become systematized by habit along special lines, such as the theatre, music, art, literature, travel, games, sports, dancing, social functions, study, forms of manual work, etc.

Recreational activities should appeal to existing interests not sufficiently stimulated in ordinary work. They should have the character of novelty and contrast, when compared with regular vocational and avocational work. They should arouse adequate but not excessive activity. They should give rise to a pleasurable feeling which tends to persist as a permanent emotional tone. Recreation should also provide for bodily exercise of a sort and kind necessary to keep the various organs of the body in good working condition.

The agreeable emotional tone aroused by activities which meet these requirements will displace the disagreeable feelings resulting from the deadening routine of work, or from fatigue, or lack of proper exercise and satisfaction of developed interests. This pleasurable feeling pervades the conscious processes involved in ordinary work, and adds to the efficiency of the efforts.

Proper recreational activities facilitate the gaining of energy during the periods of rest, and create conditions favorable to the performance of the various physiological activities which make one efficient. To be classed properly as recreational, activities must re-create, or create again, one's powers of body and mind.

Exercising interests involved in regular work, along different but more pleasurable lines, may be recreative in character, if the demands on the interests have not already been too great. The professional baseball player may find recreation in playing golf. One whose work is routine and not too fatiguing may seek recreation in matters involving close concentration of the attention and sustained mental effort, and vice versa.

The instinctive demand for recreation is one of nature's provisions for keeping alive and developing, through exercise, capacities which would otherwise die. It is also a provision for renewing the waning powers of mind and body, and keeping one's working efficiency up to the standard.

The gregarious instinct is a strong impelling force in choosing the forms of recreation. It leads one to seek his recreation in the company of others. The sympathetic instinct also leads one to seek to share the emotions of others and to share his emotions with them.

The play instinct plays an important part in the development and form of recreational activities. It, and many other subjects, taken up briefly, in this book, are discussed more fully in the author's "Psychology for Business Efficiency."

The recreation interest may be concerned with satisfying any one, or several, of the other interests previously mentioned. The end to be gained in doing a thing as a means of satisfying the recreation interest is different from the end sought in exercising the interest as part of the regular work of life. Yet one who understands the true nature and function of recreation, can often find, or make, much of his daily work recreative in character.

Almost any line of activity may be undertaken as a means of securing recreation. Many things are sold almost solely for recreational purposes.

One who is selling an automobile, for example, as a means of recreation will have to talk along quite a different line from one who is selling an auto truck as a means of satisfying the wealth interest. The recreational interest aims at novelty, contrast through change of scene or form of activity, restoration of mental and physical energy used up by serious work, and the displacement of a disagreeable or neutral, or less pleasurable state of feeling by a pleasurable emotional state; all of which tends to bring about a well-founded assurance of mental and

CLASSIFICATION OF INTERESTS 207

physical fitness. The seller of an automobile may also, of course, appeal effectively to the sociability and other interests.

The things with which the recreation interest are concerned are innumerable. They include the theater, music, literature, lines of study, art, games, travel, hunting, fishing, social activities, constructiveness applied in various manual occupations, agriculture, athletic sports, swimming, boating, etc.

CORRELATION AND CO-ORDINATION OF INTERESTS

Every one has philanthropy, politico-legal, sociability, health, education, wealth, beauty, vocation, recreation and family and home interests. He also has a moral interest which impels him to strive for self-realization along the lines of all these interests. He is under obligation to have due regard for the other interests while seeking satisfaction for any particular interest.

As a matter of fact, as a result of deficiency in natural endowment or of imperfect educational development, one may not strive for the satisfaction of his various interests in such a way that each will contribute its part, harmoniously with the others, to the promotion of his general well-being.

One may not have shown due regard for his interests in choosing and pursuing his vocation. He may be held by deeply ingrained habit to seek excessive satisfaction for certain interests. In such a case, certain interests will have been neglected so that they have not developed properly, or so that they have died out from lack of exercise.

Health may be knowingly disregarded in the struggle for wealth or pleasure. Or one may struggle according to his light, but he may not have been fully awakened (or may have gone to sleep) to the importance of the realization of his interest in certain lines. One may be alive to the importance of physical well-being, yet he may not clearly realize the importance of a certain factor as a means of impairing or improving physical efficiency.

Success in attaining satisfaction for one's vocational interest in a business, professional, scientific, artistic, political, or other career can be secured only through a long-continued concentrated process of thinking and striving.

The aim in the background of consciousness holds one continuously to a definite line of effort. The satisfaction resulting from the partial successes achieved, and the foretaste of a fuller satisfaction to be obtained from the still greater successes one believes he can achieve, spur one on to greater and more concentrated effort. One sets his eye on the end to be reached and struggles on, stimulated rather than daunted by obstacles, unrelentingly toward his goal.

The business one builds up in this way becomes flesh of one's flesh and blood of his blood. It grows to be another part of himself. Such an one is always in danger of becoming intolerant of interest in everything that does not pertain to his business. He is hypnotized by concentrating his attention on the fascinating lure of a great vocational success.

One is justified in making his vocation a major interest in life. But he is ever in danger that his vision will be so short in range and narrow in scope that he will wake up some day to the fact that he has been merely making the means for securing a living. He may come to realize, when it is too late, that he has lost for all time the greater opportunity of making a life rich in the nobler, more significant, more abiding elements of joyous satisfaction.

He has become hardened, narrowed, and unsympathetic. He has failed to gain the satisfaction to be derived from disinterestedly serving the well-being of others, from the unselfish friendship, from broad interest in learning, in literature, art, health, and life-giving recreation.

The supreme interest in life is the interest in symmetrical, harmonious, many-sided development, known as self-realization. One should be ever on his guard against exalting into a position of supreme, if not sole importance, one of the interests which should really be subsidiary to the interest in being a fully developed person. In the strenuous drive for great achievement, interests of vital importance are likely to become stunted or atrophied because they have no chance to develop through exercise. Eternal vigilance and effort, alone, will enable one to avoid sacrificing the richer, nobler self on the altar of a narrow success.

While many fail in this way, many more fail because they weakly follow the course of least resistance. They take a spineless, purposeless attitude toward life. They need to feel the spur of great ambition.

CORRELATION OF INTERESTS 211

This discussion must have made it clear that there is a very complex correlation between the interests as they habitually manifest themselves as desire in the ordinary individual.

INTEREST, DESIRE, VALUE, AND PRICE

Interests are habits of attending, thinking, feeling, desire, or aversion and striving away from or striving toward certain classes of objects.

A desire is both a painful sense of something lacking and a pleasurable foretaste of the satisfaction to be derived from securing the thing which will supply the lack. The foretaste of satisfaction is usually the more prominent or focal element in the desire. In this case the painful element will be found occupying a more or less prominent place in the margin. However, the painful element may be in the focus and the pleasure to be gained in the margin of consciousness. Each heightens the other by way of contrast. Both together give strength to the desire.

The desires have normal strength, and the values attributed to the things are normal values, when they are proportional to the various services the desired things will render in promoting well-being, or harmonious self-realization, in which all the lines of interest are satisfied in due proportion. Desires are normal when they are proportional to the intrinsic value of things. By intrinsic value we mean value in promoting general well-being. Desires and valuations are subnormal if they fall short when measured by this standard. They are inflated to the extent that they are in excess when measured by that standard. Inflated value and desire, and subnormal value and desire, are abnormal. Desire and valuation are perverted when the desire is attached to, and value is attributed to, a thing which does not contribute to well-being. Intrinsic value results from the possession of qualities which fit a thing to serve as a means of contributing to normal satisfaction of interests. By normal satisfaction is meant satisfaction, the value of which is appraised by applying the norm of self-realization.

Commercial valuation, or determining the price one can afford to pay for a thing, is arrived at by determining the balance of gain or loss in well-being which will result from the expenditure, or amount of the service, or its equivalent means of securing satisfaction, which is required to be given in exchange for the service in promoting well-being which will be gained by securing the desired thing.

The intrinsic value of a thing can not be made the basis for determining the price which may rightly or fairly be asked for it. A man of great wealth might conceivably be placed in circumstances such that a drink of water, or a supply of fresh air, or something to eat, would be of more value to him than all his wealth. In such a case, one who supplied the water, air, or food would not be justified in requiring all the man's wealth in exchange for it, if supplying it involved very slight sacrifice on his part. One who supplies a need is entitled to payment, not in proportion to the extent of the need, but in proportion to the services which must be rendered in order that the need may be supplied.

The price asked should not be in proportion to the value of the serviceable thing offered for sale. It should rather be estimated on a basis of securing a fair return for all that is contributed by the services rendered in making the serviceable thing available. Such contributions may be made in preparing the raw material and in the industrial processes of manufacturing it, in furnishing capital to carry on the industry, and ability to organize and manage it; or in transporting or selling the raw material or finished product. All who render service in any of these lines are entitled to a fair compensation. Price should be based on the cost of producing and marketing, and should allow a fair margin of profit to all rendering services in these lines. All parties to the exchange should profit by the transaction. Price not based fairly on the service rendered in producing and marketing has been inflated through control, or reduced through competition.

It is extortion, exploitation, or perversion, and is essentially fraudulent if, through monopolistic combination, or other acts in restraint of trade, or through misrepresentation, or overpersuasion in selling, one exacts an unearned increment of profit. Any unnecessary inflation of prices, or any disproportionate stimulation of interest, or any perversion

INTEREST, DESIRE, VALUE, PRICE 215

of interest, is bad business, and hence is bad salesmanship.

Governments grant to inventors a monopoly lasting for a few years, in order to reward them for the benefits they have conferred on society in making the invention and to stimulate the production of inventions.

Continual success in business depends primarily on maintaining the good will created, through lowering the cost of production and price and increasing the serviceability as much as the highest efficiency and fair returns for services rendered will permit.

The salesman should set forth clearly the normal value of the thing. It is his duty also to see that the price secured is not based on the serviceability of the thing, but that it is fairly proportionate to services rendered in making the serviceable thing available. A sale is dishonestly made when the price received is knowingly greater than the normal serviceability of the thing sold. When salesmanship secures a price in excess of normal serviceability, it is guilty of exploitation. When salesmanship secures a price which does not properly pay for services rendered in producing and marketing, it is guilty of inefficiency.

TRUTH, THE IDEAL OF SELLING

Truth, as the ideal of the Associated Advertising Clubs of the World, requires on the one hand a truthful and adequate setting forth of serviceability in promoting well-being. On the other hand, conformity to the ideal of truth demands that the price asked must be fairly proportioned to the services contributed in producing and marketing. This is the ideal to which all salesmanship should strive to realize.

"Caveat emptor," let the buyer take care, can no longer control in modern marketing. Good will is based fundamentally on honest and efficient service. The continued prosperity of a business depends on good will.

Producers and consumers, as a whole, are mutually dependent on each other. Good business has regard to the well-being of both parties to every business transaction. Benefits and the rendering of services must be mutually advantageous, in order that capacity to produce and capacity to consume may develop equally.

Truthfulness in salesmanship consists in setting forth adequately the article's serviceability to the person to whom it is sold. The truthful salesman will not understate, or overstate, or exaggerate this serviceability. He will not exact or take from the

TRUTH, THE IDEAL OF SELLING 217

customer more than a fair price for the service the article will render to him. Such truthfulness is demanded of salesmen in accordance with the moral principles which apply to all walks of life.

Truthfulness in selling is not an obligation arbitrarily imposed on a salesman. It is the only foundation on which permanent business success can be built. Efficient salesmanship must render a service which creates confidence and begets good will. It is not sufficient that the salesman honestly believes that the sale he makes will prove satisfactory. He must have such knowledge of the serviceable qualities of the thing he sells, of the general demands of business, and of the requirements of the buyer that he will be able to make satisfactory sales.

The salesman who renders the best service as a business-builder will carefully avoid making sales that do not render profitable service to the interests of the buyer. He must know the truth about the value-giving qualities of his article. Without exaggeration or distortion he must present this truth to the buyer.

The salesman, to a certain extent, relies on the confidence and good will of the buyer, on suggestion, on personality, on tactful approach, on pleasing delivery of the selling argument, on wording the selling talk in such a way that it will have great effectiveness in arousing emotional activity and volitional impulses which tend to close the sale. It is proper that the salesman avail himself of all the effective aids to selling. Such means are employed legitimately only so far as the salesman sees to it that, in making the sale, he is profitably serving the interests of the buyer.

The salesman may properly resort to an appeal to various emotions and to suggestion to action to get the buyer to accept the estimate the salesman puts on the service the value-giving qualities will render, provided the salesman's estimate is fairly proportional to the satisfaction the buyer will derive from the purchase. It is also true that the purchase must not involve undue sacrifice of other interests.

It is the salesman's duty to get a fair return for the service rendered. Getting more in return than the service rendered is worth, is not salesmanship. The seller is working a confidence game. He is obtaining money under false pretenses.

The article will render full service to the consumer, only as he has clearly in mind the service the value-giving qualities of the article fit it to render. Even if the sale is made largely by emotional appeal or by suggestion, the salesman should see that the buyer is correctly informed about the article. The salesman should make it a point to show the buyer how to get the serviceability out of the article, even if the sale can be made with less effort than that requires.

In selling to a reseller, the salesman can often make clear the best methods of merchandizing, of financing, and of creating good will. He is entitled

TRUTH, THE IDEAL OF SELLING 219

to adequate return for such service. However, the return should come in the increased profits which come from the increased market for the goods.

AWAKENING LATENT NEEDS

A market is a class of people whose needs and interests make them possible consumers, and who have sufficient means to enable them to purchase when the latent desire has been sufficiently stimulated. The market may be increased by stimulating desire; or by lowering the price so that a larger number will be able to spend the amount required to secure the satisfaction for their desires.

Men are not intuitively aware of their real needs. The existence of the need must be made clear by educational means. It is necessary to undertake consciously and systematically to develop latent capacity into an active tendency to desire.

The salesman and the advertiser perform an important educational function in creating desire. The awakened desire to satisfy the need one is thus made aware of, stimulates him to develop greater efficiency in serving the needs of others in order to get the means of satisfying his own desires. The desires thus awakened by the salesman and advertiser stimulate the men in whom they are awakened to more efficient service and thus increase production in other lines.

AROUSING DESIRE

Success in selling depends on finding what interests of the consumer are concerned with the goods so that appeal may be directed to them in such a way as to arouse desire. It will depend also on wisdom in selecting the qualities of the article which give it value as a means of satisfying desire; and on skill in presenting these value-giving qualities in such a way as to create desire for the article and arouse an impulse to buy it. The tendency to buy may be strengthened indirectly by anything which strengthens the desire. It may be strengthened directly by suggestion, or command, which stimulates the impulse more strongly.

No strong desire to possess a thing can be aroused unless an appeal is made to some form in which one of the instinctive or developed interests is manifested. When an interest exists vividly in the psychological sense, that is when one is keenly conscious of the need, all that is required to arouse desire is to show that the thing is a serviceable and available means of satisfying the need.

When the interest exists merely in the broader sense in which the fact of the need is not recognized, the salesman's task is to make clear the extent to which the well-being is concerned with the thing offered for sale.

AROUSING DESIRE

The salesman must determine whether it will be advantageous to awaken the impulse of striving away from the unsatisfactory condition of affairs, as well as the impulse of striving to gain the satisfaction to be secured by making the purchase.

When the demand already exists but the sense of something lacking is a familiar and tolerated sore, it may be necessary to dig into the tender spot and irritate it afresh, to give it potency in impelling to action. People become dulled and apathetic to old needs which they have had little hope of being able to satisfy. To arouse such a person to action one must not merely kindle the hope anew. He must reawaken keen antipathy to the evil which has come to be regarded as necessary and to be ignored. He must also awaken a foretaste of the satisfaction to be gained by securing the article. He will then have created a desire in which the impulses are both pushing and pulling one on to buy the thing.

A desire is an impulse to action as well as a feeling. The impulse is carried out into action when one sees his way clear to securing the means of satisfying the interest from which the feeling and impulse arise.

The means of satisfying a need is a want. Desire and want, and demand and supply, are similar pairs of similarly related terms.

The reader who wishes to gain more insight into the bearing on salesmanship, of processes and factors of thinking, feeling, and acting will find additional matter in the author's "Psychology for Business Efficiency." See especially the topics, "Fashion," "Leadership," "Creating Good Will in Business," etc.

The things with which the various instincts and interests are concerned will be discussed more fully in the "Psychology of Advertising." So will the various instincts and interests which may be appealed to most effectively in selling various things. See also the adapting of the selling appeal to the existing form of the interest.

SUGGESTION AND IMITATION

In the broadest meaning of the term, suggestion is the process by which a person is caused to experience an emotional state, to accept a proposition as true, or to perform an act, without giving adequately deliberate consideration to the grounds, or reasons, or evidence for or against the suggested act, feeling, or opinion thus accepted. Such a suggestion may come from the words, or expression, or acts of another person, or persons, or from material things.

Suggestion in the above sense may be known as hetero-suggestion to distinguish it from auto-suggestion. Auto-suggestion is the process by which one influences the physiological processes of his own body, or his own feelings, ideas, or volitions. Some of the applications of auto-suggestion will be made clear in the chapter entitled "Developing Character and Personality." Auto-suggestion and hetero-suggestion are both discussed more fully in the author's "Psychology for Business Efficiency."

The suggestion we are here concerned with is hetero-suggestion. The prefix "hetero" will be omitted in accordance with the general usage.

The acceptance of a suggestion is technically known as imitation. Suggestion and imitation are two aspects of the same process.

In studying suggestion, attention is directed to the characteristics or qualities which fit the stimuli to bring about the result. One also studies the processes in accordance with which the stimuli work in bringing about the result.

In studying imitation one analyzes the processes taking place in the mind of the one influenced by the suggestion. He considers the qualities or traits of character that determine the sort of imitative activity which results from the suggestion.

In order to use suggestion effectively in practical salesmanship one must understand the instincts, interests, habits and other mental processes of the customer, and must select appropriate suggestions and employ them in such a way that they will bring about the desired results.

The following discussion considers the problem of putting to practical use the suggestive-imitative process, in which the salesman employing his selling talk, solicitation, or appeal as a suggestive force, endeavors to secure the imitative response which takes the form of making the purchase.

It must be borne in mind that the term imitation is used here in the technical sense explained above. In this sense, imitative acts include all acts that are performed without giving, before their performance, adequately deliberate consideration to the reasons for or against the performance. Imitation includes all acts performed as the result of an appeal, excepting such as result from fully reasoned

SUGGESTION AND IMITATION 225

choice or demonstrated truth. One might be said to be "suggestioned" into doing such acts, if our language permitted such a term. In the absence of a more appropriate term, the word "imitative" must be used in a technical sense to describe such acts.

The imitation which follows suggestion is usually not an exact copy, or replica, of the mental state or action imitated. Generally the response to the suggestion is modified or determined to some extent by the native or acquired predispositions of the one "suggestioned." Some element of self-expression usually appears in the imitation.

Imitation and suggestion have been treated more fully in "Psychology for Business Efficiency." See also the subjects "Fashion" and "Fads" in that work.

FACTORS OF SUGGESTIBILITY

When the idea of doing a thing to which one is predisposed by instinct, or interest, or habit, gets into mind so that the attention is centered upon it the actual doing of the thing tends to follow as a matter of course, unless the act is prevented, or as it is technically described, is inhibited by another idea obtruding itself on the attention.

If one is offered something to eat between meals when he is hungry, he experiences an impulse to accept it. However, if it occurs to him that eating the proffered food will spoil a good dinner coming later, or will cause indigestion, the idea of the undesirable consequences of the act will hold in check, or inhibit, the strong impulse to eat.

The awareness of a situation which concerns the satisfaction of our instincts, or interests favorably or unfavorably, tends to bring about behaviour adapted to deal satisfactorily with the situation. Capabilities acquired innately and developed by experience come into play. The situation is handled as native and acquired aptitude have fitted us to deal with it. Responses have become largely habitual.

The feelings and emotions manifested in the behaviour of others arouse similar emotional states in those who observe this behaviour. Fear and joy and sorrow are thus aroused by suggestion. In this way the confidence, enthusiasm, and good will animating a salesman are manifested in his behaviour, and tend to arouse like states of mind in the man whom he is soliciting.

One who closely watches the acts another is performing will tend to perform similar acts. One person on the street looking up will cause many others to look up. The idea of the act tends to pass over into the performance of the act.

We are all influenced by the volitional aims manifested by those around us. The direct command and the obedience to the command is an illustration. So also the suggestion to any line of action as desired and the compliance with the suggestion. In such suggestion and compliance the instinct of self-assertion is manifested in the one who makes the suggestion, while the instinct of self-subjection is manifested in the acceptance of or submission to the suggestion.

If the one making the suggestion is looked upon as having prestige or authority, that fact tends to bring about compliance with the suggestion. The impulse of self-subjection is aroused. A state of increased suggestibility is induced. This state is aroused by those who make an impression of having power, wealth, great physical strength, large size, social standing, expertness, etc. A similar effect is produced by a reputation for intellectual superiority, or for great skill in any line, or even by the mere fact that fine clothes are worn.

Anything giving the impression that the one making the suggestion desires to promote the well-being of the one to whom it is made, tends to secure compliance with the suggestion. Anything which gives the impression that the maker of the suggestion aims to further his own selfish ends, leads the recipient of the suggestion to resent it and to refuse to carry it out. In this case the suggestion arouses the instinct of self-assertion.

Qualities which tend to promote well-being are called positive. Qualities which hinder well-being are called negative. The manifestation of positive qualities of character gives effectiveness to the appeal, and vice versa.

Certain things were mentioned above as factors which arouse the instinct of self-subjection and increase suggestibility. When the opposites of these factors are manifested, they arouse the instinct of self-assertion and decrease suggestibility.

Any state which prevents opposing ideas from being aroused through association tends to increase suggestibility. It is greatly heightened in hypnosis. Fatigue, sleepiness, and ill health would thus tend to increase suggestibility along certain lines. However, they bring on a state of general inertia which makes it difficult to influence one along most lines. The consciousness that one is not in a fit condition to deal satisfactorily with the situation may arouse an impulse to contra-imitation, or to act in a way contrary to the one desired.

Deficiency in knowledge, and lack of organization of knowledge in regard to matters involved in responding to the appeal, are factors which prevent the reproduction of inhibiting ideas through association. Hence, deficiency of knowledge, or lack of organization of knowledge, will make one more likely to be influenced by the suggestion. Stock in doubtful mining ventures is sold, not to experts in mining, but to those who know nothing about the business.

For a similar reason one is inclined to act on an appeal along the line of a strong desire. One who is sick can be easily induced to buy patent medicines. Members of one party are inclined to accept, without much evidence to support it, a story reflecting on the opposition party.

In the appeal of the salesman, several varieties of

suggestion may be co-operating to bring about the response of the man whom he is soliciting. A discussion of some of the more important will follow.

SUBCONSCIOUS IMITATION

The customer may be influenced to action by unconscious or unintentional imitation through contagion by direct suggestion. Such subconscious or unintentional imitation is brought about mainly by the effect of the suggestion on the dimly conscious marginal processes known as the subconsciousness. The suggestion produces its imitative response through the impression it makes on marginal consciousness, while the focal consciousness, which is a large factor in controlling action, is occupied with other things. This form of suggestion arouses impulses and activities which seem to be self-originated. In determining the response to the appeal they co-operate with the desires and purposes springing from the conscious deliberative processes.

Through subconscious imitation one may absorb the ideas and feelings and copy the acts of others when he has no intention or purpose of doing so, or even contrary to his express purpose to refrain from doing so. A northerner living in the south may thus unconsciously catch the southern drawl, or the southern attitude toward the negroes. We may cough, sneeze, or laugh, or yawn merely because someone else does so in our presence, or suggests it by something he says.

When those around us are depressed, discontented, irritable, or pessimistic we tend to have a like feeling. When we are mingling with happy or optimistic people, the world looks brighter to us. This sort of suggestion is often conveyed by very subtle or intangible means, such as the general tone of speaking, the bearing, the expression of the features, etc.

Through this form of imitation, the emotional state of the salesman tends to inspire a like state in the mind of those with whom he is dealing. Hence, the salesman should cultivate the habit of looking on the bright side of things. He should fill his mind with optimistic thoughts. One who appears happy and confident will tend to arouse a similar state of mind in those with whom he is dealing. He will thus favorably dispose them to the acceptance of his proposition.

In many instances the customer will respond more readily to the suggestive influences of the feelings and impulses manifested by the salesman, than he will to the reasoning of the solicitation. Feelings and impulses are directly contagious by sympathetic induction. Through subconscious induction feelings and impulses lead to subconscious imitation. The customer comes to feel a strong impulse to respond favorably to the solicitation. The impulse has been suggested so subtly that he feels it to be self-originated. Closing seems to be an act of spontaneity rather than one of self-subjection to the solicitation of the salesman.

This gives a clew to the type of man who will make the most successful salesman. The salesman who is animated by strong feelings and impulses will be much more successful than the coldly logical man, other qualifications being equal. The mere energy or industry of such a man will not make up entirely for the lack of "pep" or fire of the other sort. Of course, the feelings and impulses must be of the right sort. The salesman should be animated with the spirit of service to the well-being of the customer, rather than with a selfish desire to secure a profit from the sale, regardless of the interests of the customer, or with fear lest the customer may escape without buying.

This sort of suggestion is made partly through the tone of voice, which of course appeals to the ear. The choice and arrangement of words, the attitude or bearing, the gestures, the expression of the face, and the general appearance and behaviour of the salesman have strong suggestive force. Most of the last-mentioned factors, of course, appeal to the eye.

The salesman should take a position so that these sugestive factors can be clearly seen by the man whom he is soliciting. The salesman who retires into the shadow overlooks the fact that a great part of the suggestive force, exerted unconsciously during the solicitation, must make its appeal through the eye of the prospect.

The more clearly the man solicited can see the

salesman, the more he will be influenced by the visible manifestations of magnetic, strong, authoritative, efficient personality. Through such visible influences the salesman can inspire belief in his honesty, good will, and desire to serve. He can thus transmit to his customer his enthusiasm and the confidence he feels in his line. These subconscious suggestions accompanying the selling talk may be regarded as a by-product of the solicitation, but they are very important factors in getting the desired result.

The man who is being solicited should be able to see clearly the suggestions made by the salesman, which appeal only to the eye. However, his attention should not be centered on them, but on the selling talk, and on the sample, or the article, or the demonstration of what is being sold.

The man to whom the selling appeal is being made will unconsciously, in his bearing and expression, make suggestions which reveal the sort of an impression the solicitation is making on him. Hence, he should be seated in plain view of the salesman.

CONSCIOUS OR INTENTIONAL BUT UNREASONED IMITATION

This form of imitation is not necessarily unreasonable. As a matter of fact, the acts to which it leads are generally quite reasonable. They do not spring from a process of reasoning, but they can generally be justified by a process of reasoning. The acts thus performed come under the head of ideo-motor activity. Some instinct, or interest, or desire, is aroused by suggestion. The impulse to action accompanying it, is in the focus of consciousness, and tends to pass over into the appropriate act. The suggestion is made without a supporting reason. If it secures and holds the attention, so that inhibiting ideas are prevented from occurring, it will be carried out into action.

Sometimes a suggestion of this class takes the form of a direct command. It may be made by anything which arouses directly an impulse to action. It is then an appeal. The suggestions a salesman makes in his efforts to close the sale are often of this type.

In many of the simpler forms of salesmanship the salesman relies upon a direct suggestion for which he gives no supporting reason. The huckster cries Apples! Apples! The newsboy yells the name of his paper. Each in this case relies on an associative process to arouse an impulse to buy in the mind of the hearer. If a huckster calls out an attractive quality of his wares, he attempts to arouse the impulse to buy through a direct suggestion which creates desire.

The newsboy attempts to arouse desire and impulse to buy when he calls "All about the suicide!" He uses a suggestion aimed directly at the impulse to buy, rather than one intended to arouse desire, when he says, "Buy a Daily News." This direct command tends to arouse the instinct of self-subjection to the will of another. This merely means an impulse to comply with the expressed volition of another. Sometimes the newsboy uses still another direct suggestion as a closing feature, when he tries to put the paper in the hands of a passerby.

Things to eat, drink, or wear can often be sold without employing an appeal which arouses complicated processes of reasoning in the mind of the buyer. The salesman's task is merely to impress the attractive qualities on the mind of the customer by display and description. The clear perception of the attractive features is sufficient to arouse the impulse to buy.

The salesman often employs this type of suggestion without realizing the effect he is producing. The clerk frequently spoils an opportunity to make additional sales by asking "Is this all?" It wouldn't be much worse to ask "This is all today, isn't it?"

The clerk who asks "Is there anything else you would like to look at?" doesn't do much better.

As he closes one sale, a salesman can often lead to another by making a definite suggestion of some appropriate and particularly attractive article. For example, a clerk who has just sold a shirt could say "We have just gotten in a very attractive lot of ties. How do you like this one?" as he tactfully places before the customer a becoming tie. He thus secures an opportunity to demonstrate the attractiveness of the tie and to tell about its excellent quality and stylishness. In doing so, he will be making rational suggestions, which will be considered later.

Suggestions of this sort that are potent and far-reaching in their consequences can be made in subtle ways of which one is not fully conscious at the time. How would it affect the amount of business done on credit if the salesman regularly asked "Will you have this charged?" Consider the effect on the delivery charges of a clerk taking one of the following courses: First, suppose he asks "Will you have this sent out?" The average customer would consider the question an invitation to have the thing sent out and would answer, "Yes," though, of course, some would say "It will give me no bother. I may as well take it." Again, suppose the clerk says "Will you take this with you?" Many would say yes, and would take it, though some would ask to have it delivered. The question in the latter form might do much to reduce delivery charges, though a few might resent it as implying that the store is unwilling to deliver. If the package is one that can be carried conveniently, the best course would be for the clerk, as he thanks the customer, to hand him the package, as if he would take it as a matter of course.

Very frequently a mere suggestion will be more effective than a fully stated reason. Suppose the salesman is trying to induce a merchant to take the exclusive sale for a line. He may say, "Here is a thing which offers such and such an opportunity in your line. (Of course he would make his claims definite.) Any live dealer like you can make a great thing out of it." Some such suggestion would be more effective than to say right out, "If you don't take this, I will sell it to one of your competitors and he will secure a great advantage over you." The salesman should not make statements that may be regarded as suggesting or implying a threat. Such statements arouse a feeling of hostility.

We have been discussing the selling appeal which consists of a direct sugestion for which no supporting reason is given. It should be apparent by this time that this type of sugestion plays a large part in more complex selling appeals. This type of suggestion merges without a sharp dividing line into the type of suggestion supported by an explicitly given reason, or reasons. There is, in turn, no clearly defined boundary line between this type of appeal and the one which aims at bringing about a fully reasoned choice.

As a rule, a salesman can not make a sale by bringing about an unreflecting response to a suggestion. He generally arouses deliberative processes and encounters objections which must be overcome.

FULLY REASONED CHOICE AND DEMONSTRATED TRUTH

Under this heading comes the selling appeal which seeks to make the sale by a clear and forceful appeal to the intelligence and judgment. The salesman aims to guide the customer through a thorough consideration of the reasons for and against buying. The desire to make the purchase is to spring from adequate investigation and deliberation.

The salesman may undertake to make the sale by demonstrating the truthfulness of his claim in regard to the value of the thing he is selling, by putting the matter to the test of actual experience. By trying it out, one could thus prove that a machine can be used profitably in a certain business.

On the other hand, by considering the reasons for and against it, one may be led to the conclusion that a machine can be used advantageously. Or he may reach the same conclusion by reasoning from the experience of others in lines of business similar to his own.

In some instances the salesman can employ both logical exposition and experimental demonstration to establish the desirability of the thing he is selling. However, he rarely endeavors to conduct the customer through a consideration of all the reasons for and against the purchase. In practice he usually gives consideration only to such reasons against the purchase as are brought up by the customer.

The salesman should never undertake to make a sale when he believes there are valid objections which would make it unwise for the man to buy. He may refrain from mentioning objections which do not occur to the customer, provided he is fully assured that it will, on the whole, be to the advantage of the customer to make the purchase. In most instances, fully reasoned choice is merely an ideal to which the selling appeal aims to approximate more or less closely. This approximation takes the form of rational suggestion, which we consider next.

RATIONAL SUGGESTION AND RATIONAL IMITATION

One can rarely be absolutely sure of the correctness of even his most carefully formed opinions about the things he buys. Deliberate consideration of all the reasons for and against and demonstrably certain truth are merely ideals to which the selling talk approximates more or less closely. This approximation takes the form of a response to one of the varieties of rational suggestion. As the appeal, from the view point of the salesman, is a process of rational suggestion, so it is a process of rational imitation from the point of view of the man whom the salesman is soliciting.

Sometimes it is more effective to merely suggest the reason which will give rise to the impulse to purchase, than it is to state it explicitly. The impulse to purchase will then seem to be spontaneous or self-originated. Carrying out the impulse will then seem to be a matter of self-assertion rather than a case of subjection of self to the will of another. The following are illustrations of suggestions of this sort. "The oldest house in America." "The largest business in this line." "We make articles for the United States government." A different impulse is aroused by the following: "Makers to the king." "Made in Paris." Figurative language, if skilfully employed, is very effective in arousing impulses to action. Examples of this are "The key to success," "The highway to prosperity," "The road to happiness."

The use of suggestions which become effective only through the working of the associative processes of the mind will be discussed more fully in "The Psychology of Advertising."

It may be well here to caution the salesman against the use of bombast or over statement. Claiming too much arouses suspicion.

RATIONAL SUGGESTION

As was seen before, in some instances the sale may be brought about by employing mere suggestion. In such a solicitation there is no attempt to arouse deliberative processes and through them to create desire. Suggestion may lead to the acceptance of claims to desirability, with full conviction of their validity, without arousing a complicated and exhaustive deliberative process in the mind of the customer. Suggestions belonging to the first two classes may have an important effect in bringing about the act of closing, and in the solicitation leading up to that act.

The ordinary selling appeal consists of suggestions which become effective without the help of logical processes in the mind of the purchaser, and also of suggestions which rely on the co-operation of logical processes to make them effective. It is also true, in a very large number of cases that the suggestions play a more important part than the logical processes in making the sale. To make suggestions effective, avoid vague abstractions. Make specific statements. Employ definite and concrete ideas. See that they are clearly apprehended.

In one type of rational suggestion, in order to reinforce the impulses aroused by reasons why, a suggestion is made which aims directly to arouse an impulse to perform the act of purchasing and to make it pass over into action. Previously to the making of this suggestion, the salesman has made an effort to predispose, or incline, the mind of the customer to a favorable response to the suggestion. By giving reasons why, or by quoting authorities, he endeavors to create in the mind of the customer an attitude which will make him receive the suggestion favorably. A suggestion is then made to bring about the act of closing, to which the other suggestions predispose one.

If a suggestion is clearly and strongly made and opposing ideas are not present in mind, the impulse aroused by the suggestion will follow its natural tendency to pass over into action. The tendency to bring about compliance is strongest, if the suggestion arouse desire, or if it is directed along the line to which habit or instinct inclines. The response to the suggestion will then be purely impulsive in character and will be performed without ulterior reason or purpose for doing it. It is not founded on, or supported by reason why, or proof, or logical conviction. This type of suggestion was previously discussed.

The suggested act will be more likely to be performed if it is made to seem reasonable, and if it is in harmony with the controlling purpose dominant in the background of consciousness. In many cases, it is not necessary to get the customer to perform an elaborate process of reasoning to prepare his mind so that the suggestion will seem reasonable to him when it is made. For example, a man was desirous of buying a machine to do a certain work. The salesman mentioned a few places where the machines were being used satisfactorily. The prospective purchaser knew the people using them and believed that they would be satisfied with nothing less than first class results. He closed the deal without going into an elaborate consideration of the comparative merits of the machine. The purchaser simply followed the leadership of those who had prestige in that particular line.

In most cases the salesman must indicate the value giving qualities of the article. He must then explain, in such a way as to suggest belief, the main reasons why these qualities give value to the article.

Men do not often reason exhaustively about a thing. The salesman should not lead the customer to deliberately weigh all the reasons, for and against, which can be found.

The successful salesman holds the attention and so directs it that no competing or inhibiting idea arises with strength enough to prevent the suggestions he makes from controlling action. Men tend to accept statements made confidently and authoritatively. The reasons why, given by the salesman, will be held to be true, unless some contradictory idea occurs to prevent belief. The salesman who arouses and maintains a lively interest in his selling talk will do much to prevent such ideas from occurring. He should keep competing lines, and reasons why not, out of the mind of his customer as far as he can. By giving reasons why, and omitting reasons why not, the salesman can often induce the customer to make up his mind to purchase, without encountering serious objections to so doing.

A suggestion, contrary to the purpose dominant in consciousness at the time the suggestion is made, may be performed, if it centers attention on its self so strongly that the dominant idea lapses from consciousness. A suggestion which arouses strong feeling or emotion may thus center attention on itself.

A suggestion is more effective, if it is bolstered up with a background or fringe of ideas arousing impulses tending to reinforce it. That means that the suggestion which is the focal element will be more effective, if the ideas which have recently been in consciousness, or are still in the margin of consciousness, are of such a character that they arouse impulses to action harmonious with the focal suggestion. How this may be brought about will be explained later.

Men are inclined to act on suggestions in regard to subjects about which they know little, as reasons why the act should not be performed are not likely to occur. They follow the advice of the expert, without demanding proof, in matters concerning which they are ignorant. The man, who can give the impression that he is an expert, can readily impose on the ignorant. Stock in blue sky mining companies is sold to people who know nothing about mining, not to the experienced miners.

Selling to an expert is a different proposition from selling to an experienced buyer. One requires cogent proof before he is willing to act on a new proposition concerning matters with which he is familiar and to which he has given much thought.

The force of habit makes men shy from a proposition which resuires a readjustment or rearrangement of their familiar notions, beliefs, or habits. More than mere suggestion is required to get a man out of a rut which is leading him the wrong way. Care must be taken to make the amount of such readjustment seem as small as possible. The proposition should be presented, as nearly as may be, as offering a better means of attaining an end already recognized as desired.

A suggestion not to do a thing has little, if any, negative force. Such a suggestion merely keeps the attention fixed on doing the prohibited thing. To prevent the carrying out of an impulse to action, the idea of a course of action contrary to the impulse must be present in the mind. The word "not", in a command, does not arouse an impulse to act in an opposite way. To prevent the carrying out

RATIONAL SUGGESTION 247

of an action, it is necessary to suggest an opposing or inhibiting course of action in such a way that the attention is fixed on the idea that arouses the inhibiting impulse. To do this, one should awaken an opposing motive to action.

Some men naturally tend to do the opposite of the thing suggested. They manifest the trait known as negative suggestibility. One can almost get them to do a thing by suggesting that they do not do it. About the only way to handle such men successfully is to handle them so tactfully that they will think that they themselves suggested what you wish them to do.

If a man is ill-tempered, troubled, distressed, worried, or pessimistic, the salesman should get him into a more favorable state of mind, or wait until a more opportune time to press his business. Men are likely to be inclined to buy less freely on a day which is unpleasantly windy, or rainy or snowy, or hot, or cold. Success in selling will be affected adversely by the ill health of the customer, his state of hunger, fatigue, discomfort etc. All of these conditions will tend to affect the efficiency of the salesman, also.

Pleasure renders a man more optimistic, gives him more confidence in his own judgment, and renders him more easily influenced by suggestion and likely to buy more quickly and in larger amount. Hence the salesman should try to create a pleasurable state of mind in his customer. He should not inhibting impulse. To do this one should awaken resort to obvious flattering or jollying. These are likely to arouse offense.

To create a pleasurable state of mind in the customer, the salesman should depend upon a pleasant manner of approach and upon saying in an agreeable way the things he will enjoy hearing. Be optimistic about the prospects for business. Find some feature of his business establishment or something in his method of merchandising that is deserving of praise. Express your commendation sincerely and heartily. Create a feeling of confidence in your judgment and business sagacity. Make him realize that you are really desirous of doing what will be for his best interests.

In dealing with an experienced business man, it is well to come right to the point, and without waste of time to present a proposition which is boiled down and full of concentrated force.

In dealing with people not used to doing business in a business like way, the salesman may find it well to indulge in a little preliminary talk to permit the prospect to get acquainted with him and cause him to feel confidence in him. He may tell a funny story to get the customer to laugh with him. In this preliminary talk he can show interest in the business, or the family, or the outside concerns or hobbies of the customer. He can tell him of long continued business relations with others whom he may know, of recent business done, etc., to show that others have satisfactory business relations with the firm. He can make clear to the customer that he has a good knowledge of business conditions and prospects, and that he has a mastery of successful ways of merchandising that will help the man in his business, etc.

Adapting the appeal and the solicitation to the various interests as they are found to exist in those who make up the market will be discussed more fully in the "Psychology of Advertising."

INCREASING THE EFFICIENCY OF THE SELLING FORCE

One of the most important duties of the sales manager is to keep enthusiasm alive in his salesforce. One can be enthusiastic over a line, only when he understands its importance. Enthusiasm in a salesman is like steam in an engine. It furnishes motive power. Enthusiasm is contagious through suggestion. It oozes out in all that the enthusiastic man says and does. Its manifestation in subtle ways, in the tone of voice, gesture, expression and bearing of the salesman, arouses a like state in the mind of the customer. In religion, many men are converted more through feeling than through reasoning. Feeling has a like potency in business. A selling talk charged with good will, optimism, confidence, and enthusiasm, will accomplish what cold reasoning alone can never gain. A man's belief that the man he is soliciting will make the purchase, may manifest itself in the subtle ways explained previously and become a potent factor in making the sale.

The salesman occupies an important position in the affairs of the business world. He renders an indispensable service. He has reason for self-respect, if he has prepared himself to perform efficiently the function of his calling. If he can not be enthusiastic about the line he is selling, he had better quit it and get one he believes in, if he wishes to gain the success his ability fits him to attain.

The salesman should be given a message of good cheer and encouragement when things are not going well with him. Hauling a man over the coals, or threatening to discharge him, does not put him in a state of mind which fits him to do good work.

Credit for success achieved should be given heartily and generously. Recognition, by way of public mention and commendation of specially meritorious achievements, inspires ambition in the one so distinguished. It is also a suggestion that is potent to stimulate others to emulate the worthy act.

The sales manager who renders best service to his salesmen will be most effective in inspiring the salesmen to render efficient service.

CONVENTION OF SALESMEN

Getting the salesmen together for conference and instruction is an excellent means of improving their work. The program may include the demonstration by an expert of the best method of making a sale, of instructional and inspirational addresses etc. It will probably include a round table conference in which the salesmen exchange their views on various problems involved in selling. This develops a spirit of co-operation.

Each man is likely to put forth his best qualities in such a gathering and will take pride in making clear the things which have contributed to his success. The results attained by the more successful inspire the others to resolve to rival their achievements.

The suggestions received by each man from many sources jar him out of his ruts. He will set himself to examining critically his own successes and failures, as he hears the successes and failures of others discussed. He will acquire new ideas and will improve his methods of working.

The spirit of competing with other members of the selling force will stimulate the men to put forth greater energy and to initiate new lines of effort. To make the most of what is gained in such a convention, the sales manager must devise ways to keep this spirit alive, while the men are working separately. This can be done by keeping them informed about trade conditions and prospects. They should be told about the success of other salesmen, and how it was gained.

SALES CONTEST

Experience gained in a great variety of lines has demonstrated that a well managed sales contest is a very effective means of increasing business. The potency of the contest is easily explained. It stimulates into activity many of the strongest instincts and interests.

Among the instincts aroused by the contest are the following:—Rivalry, emulation, self-assertion, desire for approbation, fighting, acquisitiveness, coöperation with others, and loyalty to group interests. Of course some of these are active in the form of the interests developed from them. For example, the contest awakens the wealth, the vocational, the sociability, and the moral interests.

AWAKENING INSTINCTS AND INTERESTS RENDERS MORE ENERGY AVAILABLE

When an instinct or an interest is aroused the activity of certain physiological organs is correspondingly increased. The increased activity of these organs renders a greater amount of energy available for carrying out the impulses which have been aroused.

For example, the suprarenal capsules are small glands above the kidneys which secrete adrenalin and pour it into the blood. When the fighting and emulative impulses are aroused there is an increase in the amount of adrenalin secreted.

The increased amount of adrenalin in the blood stimulates the liver to give over to the blood some of the energy stored up in the liver in the form of sugar. Thus energy is furnished to maintain the increased activity of the various organs of the body involved in carrying out the fighting and emulative impulses. The increased supply of adrenalin also tends to prevent the inhibiting sensation of fatigue from becoming strong enough to check the action before the available supply of energy is used up.

In order that a sales contest may be carried on successfully, means must be employed to stimulate effectively some, or all, of the instincts or interests previously mentioned.

The instinct of rivalry is usually appealed to by offering a prize. In order that the prize may serve to stimulate all the salesmen equally, it is necessary to fix upon a fair basis for measuring achievement. A careful investigation is made to determine the amount of sales which may be justly expected from each salesman under the conditions prevailing, making no allowance for the stimulating effect of the contest. In a recent contest, credit was given as follows on a 100 per cent basis: 20 per cent was given for the exemplification of real salesmanship, 20 per cent for the greatest volume of sales at a reasonable profit, 20 per cent for the best percentage of profit on a reasonable volume of sales, 10 per cent for the largest increase of old accounts, 10 per cent for the smallest volume of rejection and the least supervision necessary from the general sales offices, 10 per cent for the smallest volume of losses, 10 per cent for the greatest increase in permanent new accounts. A definite quota is assigned to each salesman. The prize is to be given to the one who makes the greatest percentage of increase in his quota. Each salesman is kept informed as to what all the others are doing.

If the prize is considerable in amount, it will appeal to the wealth interests.

Making the achievements of each salesman known to all the others, also arouses the spirit of rivalry.

It also stimulates the sociability interest, as it makes each put forth his best efforts in order that he may stand well with others. It says to him, in effect: "The world has no use for quitters and failures. Here is a race open to all, and no favoritism is shown. The best man will win. Are you the best man?"

A similar appeal may be combined with an appeal to the sociability interest, the spirit of co-operation, and of loyalty to the business. "You have been selected as a member of this selling organization because you have shown that you have ability, industry, and high business ideals. You have helped to make this business what it is. Will you help to make it better?"

In order that the sales contest may be a success, appeals must be directed definitely and effectively to certain specific instincts and interests. If instincts and interests are awakened to activity along the right lines, the fund of energy at the disposal of the salesmen will be greatly increased. Their feelings will be kindled. Their minds will work more actively. Effort will be concentrated on the things that count.

DEVELOPING CHARACTER AND PERSONALITY

SUCCESS DEPENDS UPON CHARACTER

The efficiency of a man in any line of business depends in large measure on the character he has formed. From his character come his strength and skill in influencing men and the respect he is able to inspire in the men with whom he comes in contact. The factors which are effective in inspiring respect are traits of character manifesting themselves in subtle, almost indescribable ways, in expression, words, tone, and acts. Through suggestion, one's character impresses itself on others, whether he wishes it or not. Holding the good will of people with whom one does business depends largely upon the treatment accorded them. The treatment will be as the character is. The character can not be bad and the acts regularly good. Good character is manifested in habitually according the right treatment to others.

Character grows out of the native tendencies and impulses, the instincts and interests, which we have already discussed, as they are developed into habits by the material and social environment. The objects to which our native impulses attach themselves, and the form which their development takes, depends upon educational influences, taking them in the broad sense which includes all external influences which affect our life.

A man stamps his true value on himself. Hence, he must be what he wishes men to take him to be. No mask, or make-up, or attempt to play a part, will long prevent the inner man from impressing itself, through suggestion, on those with whom we deal. The world will take a man at the value he places on himself, provided he is not trying to float a lot of watered stock. One should strive rigorously and unflinchingly to be and do the things he ought to be and do.

Preparation for business efficiency consists in large part of developing character and personality.

Psychology is merely a descriptive science. It is interested solely in telling how the mind works and how character is developed. As a science, it has no concern to decide whether any particular habit is good or bad. To find out what traits of character are desirable, we must consult the conscience of the individual, the experience of society, educational theory, ethics, and religion. In the last analysis it will be found that the so-called bad acts are tabooed because they bring bad results. The good traits of character are so considered and esteemed because they further individual and social welfare. The best traits of character are the traits which make for the highest success.

Among the good traits of character are: honesty, industry, care of bodily well-being, cleanliness, perseverance, thoroughness, punctuality, ambition, open-mindedness, thinking for one's self, progressive spirit, leadership, confidence, courage, cheerfulness, optimism, self-control, temperance, truthfulness, obedience, courtesy, sympathy, civility, loyalty, etc. The reader can add to this list as he pleases. A little reflection will convince him that he would regard none of the virtues as traits or elements of character, unless they were habitually manifested in conduct.

To find the strong and weak points in one's character requires careful and honest self-criticism. Much will be revealed in the advice of friends, the criticism of enemies, the treatment one receives from business associates, and one's success in dealing with others. In forming his character, one should be guided by the ideal of self-realization previously discussed. He should aim at an harmonious development of character and efficiency in all lines, with special attention to the matter with which he is most concerned.

Since a man's character is made up of native impulses developed into habits of thinking, feeling, and willing, the form that his character takes is to a large extent under his control. One can change his character by changing his habits. To give up old habits and form new ones, one must resolutely refuse to yield to the tendency to act in accordance with the old habit. Just as resolutely, and unhesitatingly, and invariably, he must improve every opportunity to act along the line of the new habit he desires to form.

This is so difficult that it is necessary to get the strongest possible hold on one's self at the start. But it grows much easier to act in the new way, as time elapses and the habit gets better formed. The new way, which at first required painful effort, later becomes pleasurable. It will finally require effort to act contrary to the new habit.

The most difficult thing in forming a new habit is to get strength and resolution enough to jerk one's self out of the old rut and get a good start in forming a new one. In time the habits will become a second nature, stronger than the original nature. Do not concern yourself with the undesirable habit you wish to eliminate from your character further than to refuse to give attention to the impulse to act along that line, or to allow the impulse to pass out into action.

SELF-CONFIDENCE

To make it clear how one can develop the more complex traits of character, and attitude of mind, let us consider self-confidence, which is of the utmost importance in every line of work. A firm spirit, manifested in confident and self-reliant attitude and in decisive action, compels respectful, and even considerate treatment from others. Show fear and you invite others to impose on you. There is much truth in the saying that men can win because they believe they can win. Energy in action follows naturally from self-confidence. To develop the self-confident feeling and bearing, decide carefully what you wish to do and how to do it. Be thorough and painstaking in your preparation. Keep your purpose in view. Be on the alert for new points of view, new ideas, and new light on old ideas. You will thus acquire a fund of ideas and experience which will make you master of your line.

Give yourself good reason to think well of yourself, and then think well of yourself. You will thus develop self-confidence and initiative. Then do not stand around hesitating and irresolute. Go to work with an energy that never falters or turns aside.

Where there is a will there is a way.

Don't harbor feelings of doubt, or dwell on thoughts of inefficiency and failure. Most fears are groundless. Still more are worse than useless. By dreading a thing, you will be likely to contribute to bringing it to pass, and you will certainly increase its ill effects when it comes. Do not let your thoughts dwell on your shortcomings or chances of failure. A difficult situation once squarely faced loses most of its terror.

Overcome any tendency to diffidence or self-distrust by keeping your thoughts fixed on what you have to do, not on yourself. Keep before you the advantage and satisfaction which will come from succeeding. Study your failures only to find out how you can increase your proficiency, and then forget them. Think, instead, of future successes. Suggest to yourself frequently, "I am able to succeed. I will be self-confident. I will succeed."

SELF-CONFIDENCE

To impress your self-confidence on others, manifest in your work, optimism, courage, confidence in your ability to succeed, intense earnestness, enthusiasm, and perseverance. Work without hesitation, in a thorough and honest manner. Avoid over-tension and convulsive efforts, as they manifest weakness and involve waste of energy. Give the impression of having plenty of time to accomplish your work. Appear confident of being able to handle the situation satisfactorily.

If you wish to be a successful man, you must assume the mental attitude and manner and bearing of a successful man. The successful leader of men shows self-reliance and conscious power in his manner, conversation, and carriage. He impresses men as believing in his ability to do great things. Men have confidence in one who believes in his own ability. They distrust one who lacks confidence in his own powers to secure good results.

PERSONAL MAGNETISM

This quality is so complex in its character as almost to defy analysis and explanation. The person who is described as possessed of magnetism will be found to manifest many of the following traits. He dresses tastefully in good clothes, well-pressed and cleaned, well-kept shoes and clean linen. He is well-shaved and bathed, and well-groomed. He speaks distinctly with a pleasant and well-modulated voice. His gestures and bearing are pleasing. He shows courtesy and politeness by doing what is generally recognized as good form. He has consideration for others, and interest in their welfare, and in what they do and say. He has tact and avoids over-familiarity and weak flattery. He is cheerful, and cultivates the art of pleasing. He does the right thing, in the right way, and at the right time. He has easy confidence in himself, but is not conceited. He appears successful, shows mastery of his business and enthusiasm for it. At the same time he is interested in many other subjects, and well informed about them.

INDEX

Aesthetc interest, 197.
After closing, 86.
Approach, 17, 24, 27.
  introductory statement in, 25.
Argument, avoid, 57, 69.
Association of mental processes, 117.
  by continguity, 117.
  by similarity, 119.
  in memorizing, 125, 133.
  influence of emotion on, 121.
  process of, in education, 128.
  solicitation modifies working of, 149.
Attention
  and interest, 139.
  directs mental processes, 148.
  expectant, 146.
  focus and margin of, 145.
  holding, 36, 141.
  securing, 24, 141.
  voluntary and spontaneous, 141.
Aversion, 190, 212, 220.

Behaviour, 102.
Belief and action, 167.

Brain and mind, 111.
Character
  developing, 256.
  success depends on, 256.
  traits of, 257.
Choice, fully reasoned, 239.
Closing, 75.
  after closing, 86.
Competitors, treatment of, 72.
Confidence in salesman, 33.
  inspiring confidence, 231.
  (see also "suggestion")
  creating self-confidence, 259.
Conscious processes, classification of, 109.

Demonstration, 31, 47.
Desire, 212.
  arousing, 31, 220.
  see "interest" and "attention."
Diagnosis, 58.

Education, 128.
  interest in, 197.
Experimental psychology,
Expert, 167.
Factors which determine mental processes, 169.

INDEX

Family and home interest, 195.
Feeling out and closing, 75.

Good and bad, 192.
Good will, 51, 147.

Habit, 111.
Health interest, 197.

Ideo-motor activity.
  (see "will")
Imitation, 223.
  conscious, 234.
  rational, 241.
  subconscious, 230.
  (see "suggestion")
Impulses, arousing irrelevant, 50.
Inhibition, 150.
  (see "objections")
Instincts, 169.
  classification of, 183,
  definition of, 170.
  education of, 177.
  enumeration of, 173.
  modification of, 180.
Interest and attention, 139.
Interest, arousing,
  in approach, 25.
  in pre-approach, 21.
Interest, desire, value and price, 212.
Interests
  aesthetic, 197.
  classification of, 191.
  correlation and co-ordination of, 208.
  education, 197.
  family and home, 195.
  health, 197.
  meanings of, 189.
  moral, 185.
  morality the major interest, 191.
  philanthropy, 194.
  politico-legal, 195.
  recreation, 203
  sociability, 196.
  vocation, 199.
  wealth, 198.
  work and need for recreation, 202.
Interests and thinking, 153.
Introspection, 105.
Intuition, 59.
Intuitive judgments of character, 59, 108, 175.
Investigation in pre-approach, 19.

Judgment and reasoning, 164.

Learning,
  aims to grasp significance of things, 133.
  process of, 129.
  method of, 134.

Marketing, 94.
Means, use of illegitimate, 51.

INDEX

Meaning of things, 132.
    learning aims to grasp the, 133.
Memory and art of recollecting, 123.
Mental and physical processes, 102.
Mind and brain, 111.
Minds of others, knowledge of, 58, 107.
Moral interest, 185.
Morality, the major interest, 191.
    principles of, 193.

Needs, awakening, 219.

Objections, dealing with 27, 67, 82.
Objective and subjective realms, 103.

Personal magnetism, 261.
Personality, developing, 256.
Philanthropy interest, 194.
Politico-legal interest, 195.
Practical knowledge and skill, 11.
Pre-approach, 17, 19.
    investigation, 19, 23.
    preparation, 20.
Predispositions
    (see "instincts" and "interests")
Price, 212.
    making known the, 32, 33, 43, 74.

Proficiency, acquiring, 11, 100, 114.
Psychological moment for closing, 76.
Psychological knowledge, method of gaining, 105.
Psychology, definition of, 102.

Quality, definition of, 31, 36.
    demonstration of, 47.
    value giving, 31.

Recollecting, art of, 123.
Reasoning, 164.
Recreation interest, 203.
Right and wrong, 192.
    principles of, 193.

Sales contest, 252.
    increases energy of salesman, 253.
    motives appealed to in, 252.
Salesman, function of, 10.
    preparation of, 16.
    increasing energy of, 253.
Salesmanager, 13, 251.
Salesmanship,
    as a profession, 92.
    deals with mental processes, 14.
    definition of, 13.
    economic function of, 10, 92.
    is applied psychology, 13, 62.
Salesmen, convention of, 251.

Self-confidence, 259.
Self-realization, 183.
   gained by satisfying interests, 189.
Selling contents of this book to the reader, 7.
Selling force, improving the, 250.
Selling points,
   definition of, 36.
   putting in writing, 37.
   stating aim of, 36.
   (see also "solicitation")
Selling process,
   acquiring skill in, 11, 100, 114.
   parts of, 17.
Selling talk
   see "solicitation."
Sociability interest, 196.
Solicitation, 31.
   adapting to customer, 39.
   aim of, 17, 31.
   appeal to intelligence in, 46.
   arousing irrelevant impulses in, 50.
   brief solicitation first, 42.
   demonstration in, 47.
   effectiveness of cumulative, 41.
   holding attention and interest in, 36, 141.
   illegitimate means in 51.
   making effective, 52.
   preparation of, 33.
   renewal of, 43.
   seriousness in, 53.
   stating aim of new point in, 36.
   suggestion in, 45.
   thinking ahead in, 35.
   truth in, 45, 162, 216.
   see also "suggestion."
Spontaneous, attention, 141.
Success, depends on character, 256.
Subjective and objective, 103.
Suggestibility, factors of, 225.
Suggestion,
   and imitation, 223.
   auto, 223.
   conscious, 234.
   in solicitation, 33, 54, 146, 218, 223.
   rational, 241.
   subconscious, 230.
Sympathy, 175.

Technical terms, use of, 56.
Thinking, 153.
Truth, 45, 162.
   the ideal of selling, 216.

Value, 31.
Vocation interest, 199.

Volition, 150.
Wealth interest, 198.
Well-being, 183.
   see "self-realization"